The Butcher who Bakes

By Grace Maiolo
Cooking with Grace

FIRST PRINTED IN AUSTRALIA IN 2011 BY
THE CREATICIANS
7 PRINTER STREET
DIANELLA 6059
PERTH, WESTERN AUSTRALIA

PRODUCED AND EDITED BY HAYLEY SOLICH
RECIPES AND COMMENTARY BY GRACE MAIOLO
PHOTOS OF GRACE, RECIPES AND TABLE SETTINGS BY CHRISTINE FINLAY
OTHER PHOTOS SUPPLIED BY
MEAT AND LIVESTOCK AUSTRALIA (MEAT CUTS),
MASTER BUTCHERS LIMITED (KNIVES AND EQUIPMENT),
BIGSTOCKPHOTO.COM (PORK CUTS)
AND INDIVIDUAL PORTRAITS SUPPLIED BY SUBJECT.
PROOFREAD BY JILL BONANNO
DESIGN AND ILLUSTRATIONS BY RENEE FULTON
PRINTED BY VANGUARD PRESS, NORTHBRIDGE, WA

ISBN: 978-0-9871304-0-2

CONTENTS

PUBLISHER'S FOREWORD

When Grace Maiolo approached me to help her create this cookbook I determined it was going to be a book that she could be proud of; a book that would activate and educate people far and wide to enjoy cooking and entertaining; and a showcase of her talent as an entertainer, a butcher and a creative cook.

On the occasions that I have shared a meal with Grace, she has completely personified her name. I remember our first meeting in 2005, when I went to her home to shoot photos of her fare for Pearls Women's Magazine. Barely had I entered the house I dropped a wine glass, smashing it on the floor. Grace turned to me and smiled broadly and said, "Wow, that means we are going to have good luck."

Over the years I have sat at her table and marvelled. First at the amazing spread in front of me and secondly at how Grace manages to pull off a seamless experience. You finish one and the next appears like magic.

As we have worked together, painstakingly fussing over every detail of this book, I have seen the same level of love and care here. Grace just amazes me at how she is able to manage everything…a full-time job that keeps hours outside of what most of us would do and her other projects, like being a full-time carer, a mother of two, a regular radio guest on 6PR Radio and supporting her disabled sister.

You don't have to be a good cook to use The Butcher Who Bakes. It is intended as a resource for all people. The knives section will help you identify the right knives to use for the job and how to look after your knives. The meat section will help you know which cut of meat to buy and what to look for in your meat selections. The entertaining section will give you new ideas about how to lay your table for your guests and some meals that go together to create a dining experience. And the Easy Entertainers and Family Fillers are thrown in to give you some easy to do and practical food ideas to feed the masses.

Grace has taught me so much through this experience. I have learned how to make the meat in my casserole melt in your mouth instead of being tough as leather, and how to serve up a meal with style. I have also gained so much from Grace's tips and anecdotes which connect you to her passion for food.

I have also learned that it is okay to take shortcuts by using pre-packaged ingredients when time is an issue. Grace is VERY busy and I have often wondered how she gets up at 4am to commence her butcher's job and doesn't go to bed until after 10pm at night and yet manages to produce such great meals. If you want to know what her secrets are, you'll have to read the book but I guarantee there is something new for everyone in here.

Hayley Solich
Publisher
The Creaticians

BOB MAUMILL FOREWORD

I am delighted to write the foreword to this marvellous recipe book authored by my friend and colleague, Grace Maiolo.

Grace and I host a very popular cooking segment on Radio 6PR appropriately named, "Cooking with Grace".

Grace's wonderful sense of humour, her effervescent personality, and her love of simple recipes using local produce has earned Grace a devoted audience.

Whether it is a plain white sauce, a scrumptious bread and butter pudding, a hearty Sunday roast, or the secrets to stuffing that Christmas turkey, Grace has her special way of doing things, and the listeners love it.

What makes Grace's recipes so popular with listeners to our cooking show is their simplicity, ease of preparation, and the use of easily accessed ingredients.

I can honestly say that Grace has turned me from someone unable to make toast, into a cook capable of preparing a 3 course Sunday lunch that draws plaudits from the family.

Her book is an ideal guide for inexperienced cooks, busy people looking for easy, nutritious recipes, and people who wish to broaden their cooking knowledge.

As Grace loves to say when she presents one of her fabulous recipes, "you'll love it!"

Kindest regards and best wishes for hours of happy cooking.

Bob Maumill
Radio Announcer
6PR Radio Station

INTRODUCTION

Hi I'm Grace.

Welcome to my first edition of The Butcher Who Bakes. I've been a butcher for over 30 years and I am passionate about my work which has led me to experiment with various cuts of meats and recipes.

Working in a male dominated field hasn't always been easy as the concept of a woman wielding a knife or a meat cleaver makes some people very nervous. However, through my dogged determination I have been able to show women that you can do whatever you set your mind to and my achievement of leading the way has been a very rewarding pathway.

My inspiration for cooking came from my dear mum, who reared five children in a little country town without the modern conveniences that we know today. I was always amazed at how my mum could create a meal from minimal ingredients. We may not have had the luxuries of all the different varieties of foods, but we never went hungry.

My philosophy of cooking is that it should be an enjoyable experience, easy to prepare, and with great presentation. I firmly believe that everyone can entertain with style and present a meal that will delight their guests.

Throughout my years of experience I have learned to follow my 4P's to creating a fabulous meal.

PLAN	Thinking ahead
PURCHASE	Products that are time efficient and work well
PREPARE	Getting it all together with a minimum of fuss
PRESENT	Putting it all together for a stylish outcome that expresses your love of food

If you follow my 4P's formula, I'll throw in my 5th P and the best outcome you can get –
PERFECTION!

When I am **planning** I am thinking about what I am going to cook, considering what my guests like. Uppermost in my mind is a desire to please my guests. Then I start to put together things that mix well together, foods that are easy to prepare and present to my guests. I am not afraid to use pre-prepared foods because for me time is really important. I do encourage a lot of the younger people I mentor to start out purchasing good quality food that is already prepared so they can build their confidence in their presentation skills before they move onto starting cooking everything from scratch.

Cooking to me should be a joy and if we can take some of the labour out of that, why not?

When I am **purchasing**, it is very important to me to find products that work well, especially if they are pre-packaged. Prepared items that are fresh, full of flavour and created locally, help me and it helps local industry, so I recommend that you buy locally, if possible.

As I am quite time poor (being a busy business woman, mother, community contributor, carer and partner) simplicity and great flavour are essential ingredients in my purchasing decisions. When I have more time to devote to meal preparation, I definitely go for making from scratch.

When I am **preparing** food, I am looking for the most economical ways of putting meals together. I am thinking about the sequence of what needs to be cooked and in what order. If I can combine preparation activities for one aspect with another I will.

I am also thinking about which foods can combine well together. Also, what I can prepare the night before and then just add the finishing touches.

When I am **presenting** food, I take this part the most serious of all. I believe that presentation is the next best thing to taste. I always say that if it looks good, it already tastes good to your guests. Great presentation can cover a multitude of cooking wrongs!

Presentation says a lot about a person's character. Food that is well presented also gives guests a subconscious message that they are important and valued.

I'd love to hear your feedback about The Butcher Who Bakes. Please leave me some comments on Facebook.com/ CookingWithGrace or my website, www.cookingwithgrace.com.au.

In closing, my famous quote…"Pleased to meat you, I have meat to please you."

grace

WHAT CUT FOR WHAT MEAL?

Beef

Commonly known as 'shin beef', Gravy Beef comes from the leg and if it is cut on the bone, it is known as 'osso bucco'. Gravy Beef is best for slow cooking – stews, casseroles, and curries. By cutting the meat in smaller portions, you can guarantee that the meat will be soft and tender. Gravy Beef has a very wholesome flavour and even though it may appear a little gristly looking, it will become tender with slow cooking.

To the older generation this cut is better known as 'Bolar Blade'. It comes from the forequarter of beef. I recommend this beef cut for roasting, as it is very rich in flavour and guaranteed to be tender. Cooking 'Bolar Blade' in a baking dish with a little water keeps the roast tender and moist. No extra oil is required, as there is enough fat in the meat. An alternative that works well is to cook this cut in an oven bag. Just to create that little bit of difference, you can get your butcher to cut a pocket in the roast and add your favourite stuffing. Perfect for cold lunches.

This is my favourite cut of meat. Oyster blade steak is a very flavoursome and tender cut, so popular with all butchers. The centre of the steak appears gristly. However, when cooked, this disintegrates and becomes soft and tender and produces a beautiful flavour. Perfect for cooking on the barbeque; crumbed and also cubed for curries. Cook this cut as a whole chunk and create a tantalising roast guaranteed to be tender. Perfect cold, served with home made pickles and mustard.

continued >

WHAT CUT FOR WHAT MEAL?
Lamb

Otherwise known as lamb flaps, lamb breasts are also perfect for cutting into lamb ribs. I like to bone and roll breast of lamb with a beautiful rosemary stuffing and cut it into roulades or lamb olives. I find this is an economical cut for creating a good looking lamb dish on a budget. Roasting the lamb breasts whole in the oven works well and also gives you succulent bones to pick over.

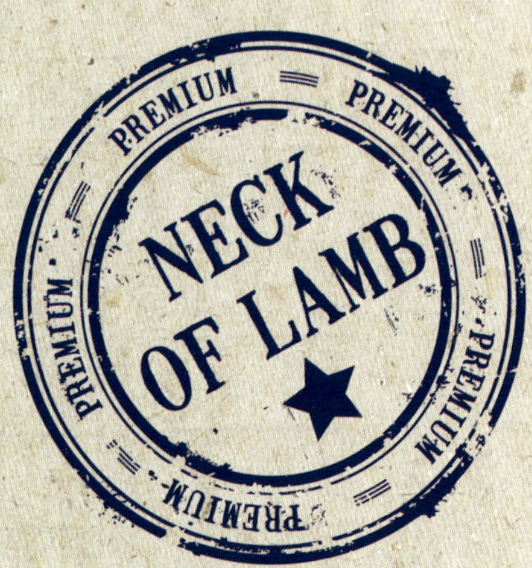

Better known as lamb rosettes or neck chops, neck of lamb is a wonderful winter warmer in dishes like casseroles or chunky lamb soup. It brings great flavour to the table and combines well with all varieties of vegetables.

Perfect for baking with a crusty coating. Or you can cut them into individual French cutlets, add some crumbs and they are ideal on the bbq or lightly pan fried.

Lamb should be pink in colour and is great crumbed, fried or grilled.

It's the perfect inclusion for mixed grills.

Choose cuts that have a little bit of fat on them, as that will ensure that the meat is tender.

continued >

WHAT CUT FOR WHAT MEAL?

Pork

Bacon rashers, known as bacon wrap.

Shortcut or eye bacon is from the eye of the loin without the tail and is perfect for the health conscious as it has little fat and is ideal for bacon and eggs or other breakfast menu items.

There is also streaky bacon, which is a fattier part of the bacon and adds a lot of wholesome flavour to dishes. This is called the middle cut bacon and is perfect for casseroles or lambs fry.

Speck is bacon that is smoked and not cooked.

The rib rashes run the full length of the loin.

Fresh knuckle of pork works well roasted or boiled for soup. It can be pickled or smoked; cut into small portions and transformed into a pork and apple casserole. This is a very economical cut of meat. If roasting, score well, rubbing salt into the skin and cook as you would a leg of pork to produce yummy, crunchy crackling.

Belly pork is absolutely perfect for roasting. Once upon a time, we used to throw out
the belly pork or send it off to make sausages. Now it has become a delicacy, not only
for it's affordability but also for the flavour and texture and the way it presents after
cooking. To get the best results, score the skin into very small crisscross segments
and pour boiling water on top and let it soak or stand for 15 minutes. This softens
the skin and opens the crisscross effect to give a no fail, crispy pork crackle. Dry belly
pork with a paper towel. Rub sea salt, combined with a little olive oil, into the scored
skin and place pork belly into a hot oven. Belly pork can also be sliced into pork
strips and cooked on a hot barbeque plate. It also makes beautiful marinated pork
strips with honey and soy or other marinades.

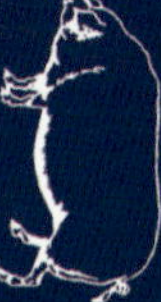

KNIFE CARE

Always remember knives are sharp – **KEEP OUT OF REACH OF CHILDREN.**

Hand wash your knives before first use and always hand wash after each use with a little detergent and a soft sponge.

To protect your knife blades corroding or staining – rinse immediately after you cut any fruit or vegetables that are acidic eg: lemons, oranges, limes, tomatoes and kiwi fruits.

Always dry your knives well after each wash and store in an appropriate place. Keep your knives away from all other kitchen tools. You risk blunting and damaging your knives if they are stored together.

Knives aren't hammers, screwdrivers or can openers.

Using them in this manner will not only damage your knives but also increases the possibility of accidents.

A simple way to sharpen kitchen knives or scissors…cut a piece of steal wool with your knife or scissors – great if you are in a hurry.

Cut food on a plastic or wooden chopping board. Do not use glass or bench tops, as this will damage and blunt knives very quickly.

Working with a sharp knife is very important as a blunt knife will damage and alter the appearance of the food. You can sharpen your knives with a butcher's steel, commonly known as a "master's dick".

Most importantly, a sharp knife is safer to use as a blunt knife is more likely to cause injury.

plastic cutting boards

"master's dick"

knife magnet   *knife block*

A knife magnet on your kitchen wall is a great way to keep your knives together, away from children and free from other blades. Alternatively, a wood block is another way to store knives safely.

My favourite accessories in the kitchen are the magic BBQ sheet, which can be used in the oven or in a frying pan. These sheets allow you to cook healthy meals and eliminates the need for oil and can be washed and reused. Most importantly they are non stick. I also recommend having a meat mallet handy in the kitchen - not just for your partner's head - but fabulous for tenderising meats with the spiky side, then flattening with the flat side.

My favourite accessories

continued >

WHICH BLADE FOR WHICH JOB?

steak knife

Steak knives are for slicing large pieces of meat or cooked roasts. The larger the blade the cleaner the cut of meat. When choosing a steak knife, choose one with a slightly curved end, as this enables you to cut more finely and to take a full cut with one movement.

boning knives (curved and straight)

Boning knives are perfect for removing large bones from legs of lamb and pork. You can also use them to trim any excess fat from joints of beef as well as slicing smaller vegetables. A curved edge boning knife allows you greater access to be able to separate the joints of the bone. A straight edge knife produces a cleaner cut and is used mostly for slicing vegetables and smaller cuts of meat.

slicing knives

Slicing knives have a curved edge and I like to use them for the larger, more solid chunks of meat. A great knife for removing fat and gristle from the joints of carcasses. When choosing a slicing knife, look for a solid grip on the handle. The rounded edge again gives you a nice clean cut.

nifty tools

There is a seemingly endless range of other really nifty tools that you can get for your kitchen. I love the melon baller, the apple and pear knife, the butter curler, apple corer and the peeler. These tools help to create an imaginative presentation out of what could be very ordinary. As I always say, presentation says a lot about a person's character.

continued >

WHICH BLADE FOR WHICH JOB?

meat chopper

Meat choppers are perfect for chopping through bones, eg chicken, ribs, soup bones etc. They are also good for cutting whole cuts of meat into smaller portions and preparing bulk meats. Fantastic for cutting up vegetables for bruschetta, ie onions, basil, garlic and tomato.

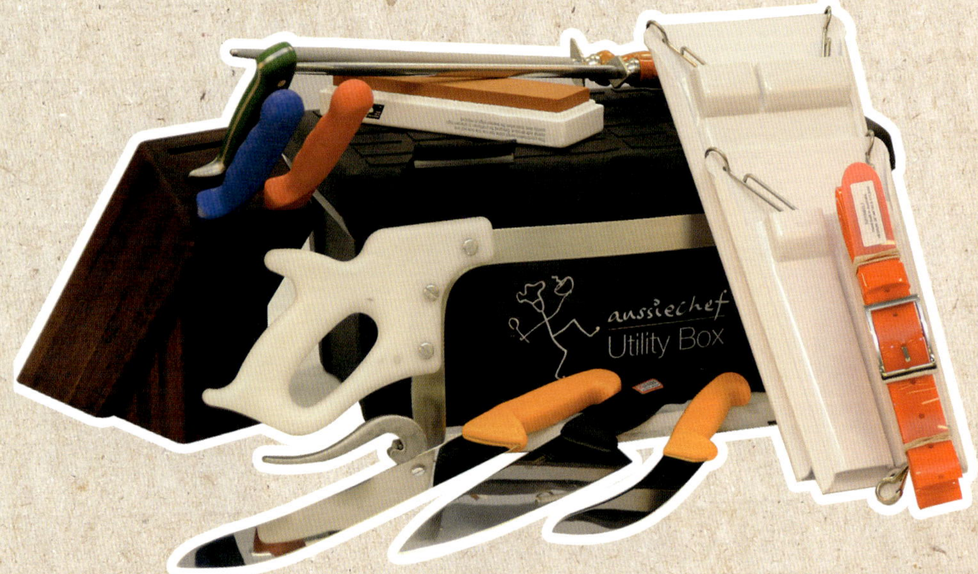

grace's knife kit

Just thought I'd share with you my kit I use for my work as a butcher. In my kit I have everything but the kitchen sink! It includes a knife pouch, a sharpening stone (another great tool in the kitchen), a handsaw for pesky carcasses, knife block and a handy carry case for when I get those emergency phone calls to rescue my rellies by helping out with some traditional Italian sausages.

WOMEN WHO INSPIRE ME

Throughout my life there have been so many women who have inspired me immensely.

In this very first edition of my cookbook, I have chosen three women who I would like to recognise and express how they have positively inspired my life and you will see them pop up in the cookbook.

I have spent a lifetime fighting for the opportunity to be recognised for my trade, against great resistance, as it is predominantly a male dominated field.

Seeing other women, who are overcoming hardships, pressures and trials to achieve their dreams gives me the courage to tackle my own and follow my heart.

These three women have encouraged me through their words, their actions and their own lifestyles and achievements. I sincerely believe if they can, I can too.

It has been the inspiration of observing these women and the personal encouragement they have given me, that has allowed me to confidently take my place.

I acknowledge them as role models in my business. Helen Reddy summed it up beautifully for me, "I am woman hear me roar!"

To these three women, I am dedicating a space in my book and a page in my heart.

DAHLIA RECHICCI

I have always admired Dahlia. She is a woman who took life with both hands, applied herself completely and reaped the rewards of her own wisdom. Starting out with very little, she became the L J Hooker top sales woman for many years running and still is one of their highest achievers. She won the respect of her peers and clients through her honesty, her integrity, her commitment, her compassion and her professionalism in representing L J Hooker.

Many said it could not be done, but Dahlia proved them all wrong and against all odds she left them for dust. Through her achievements she has provided employment for many others and has trained many representatives. In partnership with her husband, John, Dahlia has built an enduring and well renowned business.

On a personal level, Dahlia is not only a fantastic entertainer, a beautiful classy cook, and someone who keeps her house immaculate, I admire how she balances all of her responsibilities including a brood of children and grandchildren.

Christmas time and special occasions, it is nothing for Dahlia to entertain up to 100 guests at one sitting and she really does it with such style and elegance.

Many may not realise just how many hours Dahlia works in her business with John.

I have many times appreciated that Dahlia is not just someone who talks the talk, she really walks the walk and has supported me practically. Her faith in me and her willingness to share information with me, has really touched my heart. I have so enjoyed our combined dinner parties and she's humbly been my kitchen hand at many functions. She cooked chicken heads and chicken feet with such zeal for our 6PR Offal afternoon and it was an absolute winner with the guests. She really is willing to get her hands dirty to make something a success.

Dahlia, knowing you has enriched and inspired my life and for this I am a better person.

MY HAYLEY SOLICH

I believe God sends special people to our world in times when we feel a little low and maybe not quite as "together" as we would like to be.

When I met Hayley, I knew I had an in-built talent for cooking but I really needed someone to recognise it and to help me to be able to bring that talent out to share with others. Hayley saw that talent and helped me to gain the confidence to present it to the world. She also walked with me through some very difficult times and was always there for me as a source of strength and encouragement.

Hayley believes that everyone has a unique gift and talent to share and is able to recognise what that is and to draw that out in the person. Six years ago she approached me to contribute to Pearls Women's Magazine and through that opportunity we formed a lasting friendship and I started to share my cooking in print form.

I am truly amazed and mesmerized by Hayley's ability and enormous creativity, professionalism and her compassion. For Hayley, the person is more important than anything. She makes you feel so very special when you work with her. As we worked together on this book project I realised that we must get our priorities in life right, as I saw Hayley always makes time for her family, her business, and her friends, no matter how busy she is.

I see her as a compassionate mother, a wonderful friend to many people, a confidante and advisor to others. All those qualities that I admire in women, Hayley has them all.

I also love that she tackles life from a perspective of fun and a 'can do' attitude. At times this project seemed daunting, but Hayley was able to create a metaphor that showed me exactly where we were in the pipeline that helped me to hold onto the vision and to know what to do. She described creating this book as being like having a baby. It has literally taken us 9 months to grow this baby. At times we have had some false contractions, unexpected labour pains and felt the baby's movement within. She just kept encouraging me to keep pushing. And finally, it is with joy that I now am able to present my baby to the world.

For this Hayley, I truly thank you for believing in me; for being the beautiful, honest and sincere human being that you are, and I am so proud to call you my friend; and to acknowledge your amazing talents that are truly a credit to you and which the world is yet to discover. And I have included in my book so many of your favourite recipes, Chicken Parmigiana, Garlic Prawns, Warm Chicken Dip, Turkey and Rack of Lamb.

A WANDA-FUL FRIEND

Wanda Gianetti has been my friend for over 10 years. Wanda is a licensed settlement agent and I met her through business. Through the years I have observed her life and I have been amazed at her ability to run a very successful business that employs a large number of staff and how she is able to balance all the elements of her life and be so successful.

She is a gifted multi-tasker. I have seen her sitting at her desk, answering the phone, working on her computer, holding a conversation with me, whilst giving directions to her staff, all at the same time. For a woman of such little stature, she has a huge ability to influence others and has the respect of her peers in her industry.

On a personal level, Wanda is what I call my gadget lady. In Wanda's kitchen, there are so many gadgets that I have never come across and her kitchen is so well organised. Wanda designed her kitchen herself and it has all the hallmarks of a creative, thinking woman. Everything is at her fingertips, yet when it comes to tools to measure ingredients, there are none. Why? Because Wanda is what I call a professional "eye-cooker". She doesn't have to measure, because she can look at something and know it's weight, size and the quantity required to produce a good end result.

Her signature dish, Pizzoccheri, was a new experience for me. It is a peasant dish of the past, cooked in many parts of Northern Italy, made from buckwheat and can very easily be classed as a vegetarian dish.

Wanda cooked this for me while I was there. I was taken by her style and flair, and from start to finish was only 40 minutes. I was truly inspired by how Wanda juggles her busy lifestyle and her many and varied responsibilities. Every month she has a family get together where she cooks for a multitude, plus she also manages a large annual corporate ball event where her creative talents really shine. She just amazes me with her energy, warmth and sincerity, but most of all her willingness to help her friends.

That's why I call her my Wanda-Ful Friend.

WANDA'S RICETTA FOR PIZZOCCHERI ALLA VALTELLINESE
[BUCKWHEAT TAGLIATELLE]

Prepare

1. Bring a large pot of salted water to the boil and add the potatoes and silverbeet.

2. When potatoes are half cooked (approx 7 mins) add the pizzoccheri.

3. Add the spinach when nearly cooked.

4. Allow the 50 gm butter, onion, garlic, spice and sage to saute very gently (do not burn). The butter must be golden brown and the onion/garlic transparent.

5. When the water comes to a boil and after 10 mins taste the pizzoccheri. They will appear al dente (soft), there is a raw quality due to the buckwheat.

6. Warm a large serving bowl (Wanda usually puts boiling water into the bowl to warm it).

7. Drain the pizzoccheri and vegetables quickly and do not let them go cold.

8. Put one layer into the bowl and generously add the grated parmesan cheese. Add 5 slices of butter (not in one heap) and add a generous amount of the grated fontina.

9. Continue until finished and then on the very top after the cheeses are added, add the melted butter.

10. Mix all the ingredients together well and serve on warm plates.

Purchase

500 gm Pizzoccheri (available from continental delis or RE stores)

5 medium potatoes cut into medium sized cubes or rough pieces

1 bunch silverbeet with green and stalks cut into 2.5cm pieces

2 bunches English spinach chopped into 5cm pieces

250 gm unsalted butter sliced thinly

200 gm good grated parmesan cheese

200 gm grated fontina cheese

2 medium onions grated or chopped, not sliced

4 medium sized garlic cloves finely chopped

5 large sage leaves

Salt and pepper

½ tsp mixed spice

Chilli powder or pepperoncini thinly sliced

Present

Lovely served with crusty bread.

When you have made this meal once, you can judge for yourself the balance of ingredients or substitute other cheeses or greens, as Wanda has never been one to measure exactly, but goes by taste and what her mother taught her.

SPRING TABLE SETTING

Plan

To achieve a stunning table setting, you don't have to go to a lot of expense and you can prepare things in advance. A little bit of imagination goes a long way. Utilise what you already own. Mix and match to achieve a unique look.

Choose a colour scheme and stick to it.

Think of ideas that your guests would like…doesn't have to be complicated. A simple thing like remembering their tastes, likes, dislikes and any food preferences says a lot about you as a host or hostess.

For example, my friend Hayley loves bright colours. When she graces my table, I make sure that her favourite dish is on the menu and the table matches her bubbly personality. Our spring table setting reminds me of her.

Setting the table the night before takes a lot of pressure off you on the day. If you have the opportunity, try it.

Purchase

White table cloth

Spring flowers
(real or imitation will work well)

Bright coloured serviettes,
mixed with white

Tumblers, liqueur and wine glasses

White salt and pepper shakers

White dinner set

Coffee set, for short black

Present

The table cloth doesn't have to cover the whole table. You can have a shorter cloth and place food on chopping boards or pot stands on the uncovered table to create a warm look, especially if you have a lovely wood table.

By placing serviettes in glasses, you give the table height. Levels are really important to consider in presenting your table. Try for different levels, even when serving. You will notice that I have deliberately chosen short tumblers and tall wine glasses to create this effect.

When hosting small dinner parties for four or six, I always like to place the entrée as a centrepiece, as it focuses everyone in and provides a great topic for conversation. The warm chicken and corn dip works well for this, as it is an informal entrée, where my guests can experience the joy and fun of sharing this mouth watering dish.

From my experience gained from over 30 years of entertaining, I have observed that by sharing an entree, people feel more comfortable if they have control over the amount they eat, rather than feeling like they have to consume everything on the plate. This allows my guests to pace themselves through all the courses. At my table there is always an abundance of food and no-one leaves my home empty handed.

Purchase

1 lge Italian or cob loaf

500 gm cooked chicken

1 can creamed corn

1 cup tasty mayonnaise

1 small jar salad cream

1 cup chopped spring onions

Paprika

2 cups grated tasty cheese

Salt and pepper to taste

Prepare

1. Set the bread to one side and in a large bowl mix all other ingredients together.
2. Cut off the top of the bread loaf to make a lid (see thumbnail).
3. Scoop inside of bread to form a boat for the dip.
4. Place bread on a baking tray lined with baking paper.
5. Fill the boat with the dip mix.
6. Place the lid next to the bread.
7. Sprinkle the mixture with paprika.
8. Bake in a hot oven on 180° for 15-20 mins.
9. Remove from the oven and cut the lid into pieces and reassemble lid on top of the dip.
10. Garnish with chopped spring onions.
11. Serve on a warm plate as a centre piece for self service.

Present

You repurpose the bread you pull out of the loaf for stuffing or scoop out in big pieces and toast with your loaf for dipping pieces or freeze for use in other recipes.

For entertaining this is a great dish to serve at parties or for a bring and share meal.

You may substitute tuna for chicken. This is a great way to utilise any unused bread.

You can also use smaller bread rolls to create individual serves using the same method.

GRACE'S FAMOUS CHICKEN RISSOLES

Purchase

500 gm chicken mince

2 eggs

1 pkt your favourite breadcrumbs

2 cloves garlic finely chopped

¼ cup parmesan cheese

Salt and pepper to taste

Fresh parsley finely chopped

Prepare

1. Combine all ingredients in a bowl and mix well.

2. Roll into rissoles.

3. Gently fry in a hot frying pan with a little oil.

4. Cook evenly on both sides, until golden brown.

5. Serve with your favourite sauce and a sprig of parsley.

Present

This recipe is perfect to make miniature meat balls or add to your favourite spaghetti.

Also makes a good mixture for chicken burgers, served between two thick toasted Italian bread slices.

The recipe is plain and simple and well loved. Many of my butcher mates have adopted this recipe for their butcher shops.

CRISPY SALAD

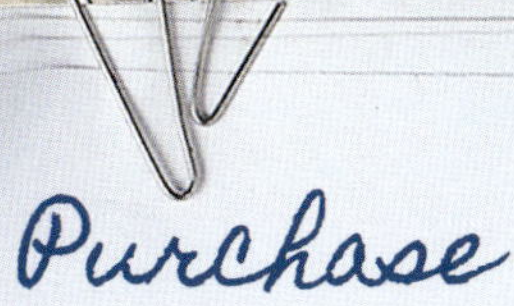

Purchase

2-3 different varieties lettuce

Cherry tomatoes or whole tomatoes cut into 4 to 6 pieces

Cucumber

Red onion

Red capsicum

Black pitted olives

Carrot

Prepare

1. Wash and drain all vegetables.

2. Cut tomatoes into 4 to 6 pieces or use cherry tomatoes.

3. Peel and slice the red onion.

4. Partially peel the cucumber to create a stripy effect or using a fork, drag prongs along edge to create stripes.

5. Peel and thinly slice carrots into rounds.

6. Cut up a red capsicum into long strips to decorate the top of the salad.

7. Place lettuce leaves into a fancy white or glass bowl.

8. Arrange tomatoes in the centre of the salad.

9. Place onions, carrots, cucumber, and olives decoratively.

10. Garnish with red capsicum.

Present

Dress the salad at the last minute or serve a selection of dressings on the side.

I suggest keeping your dressing simple. Use good olive oil, a little cream balsamic vinegar, rock salt and ground black pepper.

Salads can be prepared prior to the dinner party, covered in cling wrap and stored in the fridge.

To achieve a great looking salad, use a variety of mixed greens and add colour through your tomatoes, carrots, onion, and olives.

CARAMELISED PEARS

Purchase

8 firm, crisp pears with stalks on

2 cups sugar

2 cloves

1 cup water

Chocolate topping

Icing sugar (for dusting)

Prepare

1. Peel strips off pears (stripy finish) and set aside.
2. In a deep saucepan, place sugar, water and cloves.
3. Heat until dissolved and most of the liquid is evaporated.
4. Place peeled pears in saucepan and gently cook, basting often.
5. Prepare a large serving plate by drizzling chocolate topping to form a swirly pattern.
6. When pears are tender remove and place on a serving plate with stalks upright.
7. Pour any excess liquid over the pears.
8. Decorate with strawberries and green leaves.
9. Drizzle with extra chocolate topping for effect.
10. Generously dust the pears with icing sugar.
11. Serve immediately.

Present

Great served with a scoop of ice cream, mascarpone cheese or grated chocolate.

Use mint or any green edible leaf to decorate.

BLACK AND WHITE SETTING

Plan

A setting for two. I have chosen a black and white theme, but could be any colour scheme.

Purchase

2 boldly checked tea towels

Serviettes to match colour theme

Salt and pepper shakers

Wine glasses

Tumblers (for water)

White and black plates
(or coloured to suit your theme)

Decorative serviette holders
(swans used)

Cutlery

Present

With little expense, you can create an imaginative table presentation.

Substituting a tea towel for placemats or table cloths, opens up many more options for your table setting.

By sticking with a black and white theme, you create a canvas for the rich colouring in your foods. I think you'll agree the prawns look amazing against the black and white.

By using larger plates, you can create a restaurant feel in your own home.

If you stick with the one colour for your plates, you can mix and match across sets. For example, my pantry is full of white plates and serving dishes of all different shapes and sizes, picked up from "reduced to clear" baskets and mixed and matched. You will notice the fan plates used for the prawns (see next page). I picked up a set of four which were part of a set of six which had two missing. I got them for a song and they are perfect for this setting.

Also, the long black plates, which look like glass, are actually heavy plastic serving trays.

SKEWERED PRAWNS ON A BED OF RICE

Purchase

20 raw prawns

4 skewers (soaked in water)

1 bottle of satay marinate

1 lemon cut into wedges

Parsley for garnish

Prepare

1. Marinate prawns in satay sauce. Can be left overnight for best results.

2. Add 5 prawns to each skewer.

3. Fry with a little butter until prawns are cooked (turn orange).

4. Serve on a bed of rice.

5. Garnish with a wedge of lemon and a parsley sprig.

Rice

2 cups rice

1 tsp Paprika

1 tsp dried dill

Prepare

1. Boil rice, strain and let rest.

2. Mix paprika and dill in with rice.

Present

For those who like it quick and easy (like me), you can use pre-prepared products. I use Global Seafood prawns on skewers, they are already skewered and marinated. I find it's convenient, tasty and an impressive option. You can also use pre-cooked rice to keep the preparation time down.

By using pre-prepared prawns and rice, you can have a delicious entrée ready in 5 minutes, perfect for unexpected guests or when you are on a time budget.

For me it makes sense to use pre-prepared products if they taste good and you get a great end result every time.

Purchase

2 whole skinless chicken breasts

1 bottle your favourite tomato cooking sauce (I use Calabrese)

1 cup bread crumbs

Salt and pepper

1 cup shredded tasty cheese

4-6 spring onions finely chopped

250 gm diced bacon or ham

Paprika to garnish

SALAD

Mixed green leafy salad mix

Cherry tomatoes

Prepare

1. In a bowl, combine cheese, chopped spring onions and the ham/bacon cut into small pieces and mix together and set aside.
2. Butterfly the chicken breasts (slicing through the middle but not right through, so the breast opens out like a butterfly)
3. In a plastic bag (freezer bags work well), place bread crumbs with cheese, salt and pepper.
4. Place chicken breasts in the bag and press crumbs onto the chicken on both sides. (There is enough moisture in the chicken to make the crumbs stick.)
5. This method eliminates a lot of mess and enables you to firmly press the crumbs to the chicken.
6. Add and heat a little oil in a frying pan.
7. Brown schnitzels on both sides, partially cooking.
8. Place on paper towels to drain oil.
9. On a baking tray lined with baking paper, place the chicken breasts.
10. Spoon the tomato cooking sauce on top of each schnitzel, with the majority in the centre of the breast.
11. Spoon cheese, spring onion and ham mix on top.
12. Sprinkle with a little paprika and bake in a preheated oven (180°) for 20 minutes.
13. Serve with Crispy Green Salad in a bowl and dressing of your choice.

Present

By pre-cooking the chicken breast, it cuts down the oven time, saving energy and ensuring the chicken is cooked right through.

Baking paper is always a winner in my kitchen because it saves on cleaning time, eliminates food sticking to the baking tray and reduces the use of oil.

If you like it cheesy, sprinkle a little more when you take it out of the oven. The heat from the chicken will gently melt the cheese, leaving a glossy look.

You can also serve the crumbed chicken schnitzel fully cooked without the topping and it's a great left over as it tastes good cold.

If you are short on time, pre-cook your schnitzels the day before, then finish off with the topping and time in the oven.

You can also prepare your schnitzels for cooking and freeze them, so it may pay to do a batch and save some for another time. You can also freeze the topping and it keeps well.

If you are a 'thigh man', you can use boneless thigh fillets and tenderise them (with a kitchen mallet) to make them thinner.

DEMI MERINGUE WITH MIXED BERRIES

Purchase

Small meringue shells with wells

1 punnet strawberries

1 bottle strawberry topping

2 tbsp sweet sherry

1 cup mixed berries

1 bottle chocolate topping

Icing sugar for dusting

Prepare

1. Chop and mix all berries together in a bowl.
2. Add sherry and strawberry topping.
3. Mix well together.
4. On dessert plates, drizzle strawberry topping and place meringues evenly on plate.
5. Generously scoop mixed berries into the meringue wells, overflowing the meringues.
6. Lightly dust with icing sugar and serve immediately.

Present

Preparing the berries ahead of time will allow them to marinate in the sherry enhancing the flavour.

Meringues are a great standby, as they last a long time in the pantry and can be easily prepared for a great dessert and you have to love that there is no baking involved.

You can also serve it with unsweetened or whipped cream.

This dish looks magnificent served on rectangular plates, as you get the contrast between the round lines of the meringue and the straight lines of the plate. If you choose to use a round plate, arrange the meringues in a circle, rather than a line.

How to sort out a wine induced headache - rub half a lime on your forehead and the throbbing will go away. (Works well for me)

DEMI MERINGUE WITH MIXED BERRIES

BLUE TABLE SETTING

Plan

I like to match my food and colours together when I choose my table settings and my menu plan. In this setting, I have chosen a lighter shade of blue because I find blue so refreshing. I am matching that with the lightness of the bruschetta entree, which gets the taste buds working.

If I am entertaining in summer I tend to use the lighter, brighter colours because they reflect the season.

When I use a lighter coloured table cloth, I go for a darker shade of that colour for my serviettes as it lifts the table setting. Variations of the same colour work really well.

In this setting I'm using a light print on the plates to match the table cloth. Once again I am using the tall and short glasses to give variations in height.

When guests arrive and see the table laid out they immediately recognise that you have gone to a lot of trouble and it gives them a sense of anticipation about the meal.

The centrepiece I have here is always a conversation starter in my house as guests try to work out it's purpose. I have been known to use it for flower arranging; serving prawns, sliced fruit, chocolate fondue sticks; and just as a centrepiece where I have added water and dye to match the table setting. I've also used it to hold personalised notes as a lucky dip for my guests. It really is a very useful piece that I picked up from a relative. Most people would overlook it but I saw it's potential and it's incredible value as a flexible centrepiece for creating mood and conversations.

Purchase

Short tumblers

Blue and white serviettes

Cutlery

Salt and pepper shakers

Serviette rings

Serving dishes suitable for pasta

3 plates for the entrée and main meal

Parfait glasses for dessert with square saucers

Long spoons

Cup and saucer for short black coffee

Side dish of fruit

Butcher's paper (as placemats)

Present

I love to use Butcher's paper because:

1. It minimises your clean up process.

2. Guests are delighted to write messages on the paper and it provides an amusing talking point.

3. Looks functional.

4. White blends with any setting.

5. It's economical.

Bruschetta is a substitute for plain bread rolls and complements the main meal.

Adding chocolate sticks and a strawberry to a simple trifle, lifts it out of the ordinary and into the professional looking arena. I can't stress strongly enough how important the little touches are to making the big picture look beautiful and inviting.

RECIPE
FRENCH ONION DIP

Purchase

FRENCH ONION DIP

250 gm packet cream cheese at room temperature

40 gm packet French onion soup mix

2 tbsp chopped chives or fresh parsley

Sprinkle of paprika

Prepare

1. Combine all ingredients except the paprika in a bowl.
2. Mix well.
3. Serve in a small dipping bowl and sprinkle with a little paprika.
4. For stronger flavour, add extra French onion or a little crushed garlic.

TABLE CONDIMENTS

Long bread sticks

Black olives

Toasted garlic bread toasties

Tomato for garnish

Sprig of parsley

Present

Use a wine glass to stand up the bread sticks and create height in your table setting.

You can use green or black olives or both for variety.

Adding tomato gives it a splash of colour.

Serve on a long serving dish or tray.

You could also consider adding dried fruit to the platter, eg prunes, apricots etc which help your bowels.

Serve as a centrepiece so your guests can interact and enjoy with pre-dinner drinks. Once again, your guests can control their level of consumption and it's not a heavy entrée, which complements the heavier main meal. Great for getting the palate ready for the marinara treat.

If you have had an issue with your soup or stew being too runny, you can thicken it with a little instant whipped potato, until you get the required thickness.

SPAGHETTI MARINARA

Purchase

500 gm thin spaghetti

½ cup parmesan cheese

Fresh parsley

Olive oil

2 cloves garlic

500 gm frozen packet marinara mix

2 jars tomato cooking sauce

1 onion finely chopped

Prepare

1. Using a large deep pot, ¾ fill with water and place on stove. Add a tbsp of salt and bring to the boil.

2. Finely chop parsley, onion and garlic.

3. In a wok, place two tbsp oil and add the finely chopped cloves of garlic.

4. Then add the finely chopped onion and cook until tender.

5. Once onion is tender, add the finely chopped parsley.

6. Add the tomato cooking sauce to the pan and mix well, bringing it to the boil. Allow to cook for 5 mins and reduce the heat to let simmer while the pasta is cooking.

7. Once the water is boiling, submerge pasta in the water. Stir and cook until al dente (pasta is firm but cooked) – approximately 8 minutes depending on the thickness of the spaghetti.

8. Once pasta has been cooking for two minutes, increase the temperature of the sauce to high and add the marinara mix.

9. Stir and cook uncovered until pasta is ready.

10. Drain pasta and place in deep serving bowls for individual portions or a deep dish for self-serve.

11. Pour most of the marinara mix over the pasta. Gently mix the marinara with the pasta by lifting the pasta with a spaghetti scoop. Place remaining marinara mix on top.

12. Sprinkle with a good serve of parmesan cheese and a little extra fresh chopped parsley.

13. Serve hot.

Present

For the cooking sauce, combine two different types. I use marinara or calabrese.

Using the finer pasta will save you time and the flavour will absorb through the pasta more easily giving a tastier meal - more tomato and marinara and less pasta flavour.

You may want to consider adding extra large prawns to the mix, which makes for a better presentation of the final product.

If you choose to add mussels, that is half mussels with shells, that gives the meal that very European look, with a restaurant feel.

Fish pieces may also be added in the very last minute of cooking. This gives a more fishy flavour.

Serving this meal with a great white wine will complement the flavours and also the addition of some garlic bread on the side would be a winner.

EVER SO QUICK TRIFLE

Purchase

1 jam sponge roll

1 green and 1 red ready made jelly cup

1 tub Brownes thick custard

1 small tub double thick cream

4 strawberries

Mascarpone cheese

Grated chocolate

Prepare

1. In two large, deep wine glasses, place two custard scoops and arrange four slices of jam sponge in each glass.
2. Add half the jellies and pour a little cream over the top. Repeat this process until glasses are full, finishing with custard on top.
3. Add two scoops of mascarpone cheese to the top of each trifle.
4. Cut strawberries in half and place on top of mascarpone.
5. Grate a little chocolate on each and place in the fridge until ready to serve.

Present

This dessert is able to be prepared in advance and you may add your favourite liqueur or a little sherry in each layer.

If you want to prepare a bowl instead of individual serves, simply double the ingredients and add fruit to the final layer.

Any types of cake would work well with this.

This is a great way to use up any leftover cakes and it doesn't have to be the one type of cake but can contain a mixture.

Most products are readily available on the shelves of your local supermarket and this is a great and easy dessert when catering for unexpected guests. I have many times opted for trifle when guests have announced their imminent arrival because it is always well received.

TODAY'S MENU
GARLIC
PRAWNS
TODAY'S MENU
FILLET
STEAKS

APRON SETTING

Purchase

1 butcher's apron or striped butcher's material

Wood pepper shakers

Pottery wine goblets

2 black trays

2 white plates

Wooden handled knives and forks

2 garlic prawn ramekin dishes

Wooden serviette holders

Wooden bread serving dish

Butcher's paper

2 short black pottery coffee cups and saucers

White serviettes

Wine glasses

Wine bottles – white and red or you can choose

Present:

What works well with this setting is some novelty accessories (ie I've used the pig and the cow to display what's on the menu), creating a steak house feel to the table setting.

This is a very masculine setting, perfect for entertaining the male in your life as it will appeal to his masculinity.

Also I've chosen a meal that is very satisfying for a male. As they say, "Feed your man meat!" and that's not just 'cause I'm a butcher (works well for me all the time).

I've chosen black for the masculine and white to pick up the stripe in the apron and to contrast the setting.

Did you know...

A roast with a bone in will cook faster than a boneless roast. Why? Because the bone carries the heat to the inside of the roast a lot quicker.

GARLIC PRAWNS

Purchase:

1 kilo shelled, de-veined, raw King prawns, tail on

250 gm unsalted butter

6 large cloves of garlic

2 tbsp good olive oil

½ cup Fresh parsley finely chopped

Salt and pepper to taste

1 tub of thickened unsweetened cream

Paprika

Prepare

1. In a deep frying pan, place the butter and oil and heat until butter is melted.

2. Finely chop the garlic cloves and add to the pan.

3. Add finely chopped parsley.

4. When butter is sizzling, add the prawns and stir until the prawns have changed colour (the tails should turn orange in colour). Should take about 3-4 mins only.

5. Sprinkle with paprika.

6. Add the tub of cream to the pan, covering all the prawns and stirring to combine with the pan juices to create a sauce.

Present

I choose to mix the oil and butter together so that the butter doesn't burn.

Serve into individual ramekins that have been heated.

I like to serve with a wedge of lemon for two reasons…it is a nice colour splash and it also adds a little zest to the flavour.

It is important not to overcook the prawns. This is why I choose prawns with tails on, as they act as a visual clue to know when prawns are cooked.

The aroma of sautéed onions or fried garlic will make your kitchen smell wonderful and homely just before your guests arrive.

Purchase

500 gm eye fillet steak

2-3 cloves of garlic

Fresh parsley

Salt and pepper mix

Cream of balsamic vinegar

Worcestershire sauce

Barbeque sauce

Tomato sauce

½ cup olive oil

Small dinner rolls

Prepare

1. Cut the bread rolls in half and place on a baking tray. Scoop out the inside of the bread roll to create a small boat. Toast in the oven. (Put the scooped out bread into a freezer bag and save for stuffing or other.)

2. Using a very sharp filleting or steak knife, remove any sinew or fat from eye fillet.

3. Slice the eye fillet as thin as possible, always slicing against the grain.

4. Cut each slice into very thin strips.

5. Finely chop up the fresh parsley and garlic.

6. In a bowl add the oil (choose a good quality olive oil) and also the parsley and garlic.

7. Add sliced meat to the bowl.

8. Add salt and pepper. Add ¼ cup of each sauce and ¼ cup of vinegar, mixing well, then taste. If required, add more of your favourite sauces.

9. Place in a glass serving dish.

10. Remove toasted bread rolls from oven and serve on a platter with the Jappy Beef in the centre and bread rolls around the outside.

Present

Eye fillet is the best cut of meat to use for this dish and it needs to be good quality meat.

To get the best results for this dish, the thinner the meat slices the better it will taste.

To make it easier to cut the beef, partially freeze the meat. This enables you to have more control in the cutting process.

Although this is a raw meat dish, it doesn't taste like raw beef. The juices from the marinade permeate the whole meat and every time I serve this people are amazed at the taste sensation. It's a great conversation starter.

I have chosen this as a main course but it is equally as good as an entrée or as an entertainer's tray dish.

This was an experiment that went really well. I created it one day and trialled it at a dinner party without letting my guests know it was raw meat. After the bowl was cleaned out, I chose to let the guests know what they had actually eaten and the reaction was they all wanted the recipe before they left.

This works really well if you prepare the night before and allow it to marinate for a longer period.

If you find it difficult to slice meat thinly for particular recipes, for example, stir fries, stroganoff, etc, partially freeze and it will slice so much more easily.

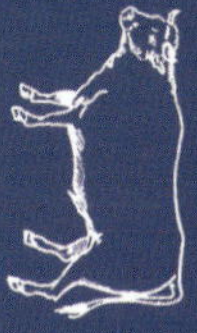

PROFITEROLES

Purchase

1 tray profiterole shells

1 sleeve prepared vanilla custard (ready for piping)

Icing sugar for dusting

1 bottle of Ice Magic chocolate sauce

Strawberries to garnish

Flaked almonds

White paper doily

Prepare

1. Make a hole in the back of each profiterole and fill completely with custard.

2. In an open glass dessert cup, squirt chocolate to cover the bottom of the cup.

3. Arrange profiteroles in a stack and dust with icing sugar.

4. Pour chocolate sauce over profiteroles.

5. Serve with a strawberry on top and flaked almonds.

6. Set glass on a square plate with a white paper doily and a dessert fork.

Present

Profiteroles can be served warm by warming the custard and chocolate.

For quick and easy convenience, it's great to have a packet of profiterole shells in the pantry for unexpected guests.

This is a classy treat that looks great and is so quick and easy to prepare as all the ingredients can be obtained pre-prepared.

If you would like to serve this at an afternoon tea, place the profiteroles on a large serving tray, dusting with extra icing sugar and garnish with strawberries. Leave out the chocolate as it is too messy.

Profiteroles do not keep well, so should be prepared and served on the same day. Refrigerating tends to soften the profiteroles, spoiling the texture.

GREEN AND WHITE SETTING

Purchase

Green checked placemats

Cutlery

Ornate champagne glasses in varying sizes

Water tumblers

White salt and pepper shakers

Green and white serviettes

Square bread and butter plates

White paper doily placemats

Divided plates

Present:

The ornate glasses add some sophistication to the setting.

The integration of the green and white serviettes complements the white plates and green checked placemats.

This entrée gives the guests variety and the choice of divided plates is to enable guests to select from the various offerings without having to mix foods.

This is the perfect setting for a girlfriends lunch or intimate, romantic lunch for two.

I intentionally chose to make the meat and vegetable snacks without using bread, as bread can be quite filling. The main course in this meal plan is already heavy.

When you are creating your platter of mixed nibbles, remember to create different height levels as this really adds to the presentation. By rolling the salami and standing it up in an egg cup I have added height to the plate, making it easier for my guests to access and it looks wonderful.

The inclusion of a little decoration on the platter – I've chosen glass grapes – just adds a finishing touch and communicates my desire to please my guest.

Before you start cooking, prepare as many ingredients as you can. For example, open tins, measure, slice, grate, chop ingredients and line and grease any dishes you are going to use.

Purchase

FOR SNACK STACKS

Tomatoes

Sliced meats
– salami, ham, polony, chicken

Cucumber

Parsley to garnish

Tooth picks

Cheese slices

Prepare

1. Create a stack by layering meat, cheese and vegetables.

2. Cut the stack into four sections.

3. Secure with a toothpick, adding a vegetable to the top.

4. Garnish with parsley and serve on a long serving dish or tray.

5. It is important to mix the colours of the meats and vegetables to create an interesting layered finish. I have chosen green and red vegetables, to complement the table setting.

6. When choosing meats, try to go for the rounder cuts, as you will find it easier to cut into fours.

7. Choose the slightly thicker cuts.

Prepare

1. Choose a serving plate that can display all the nibblies attractively.

2. If serving on a flat dish, create varying height levels by adding food in bowls or cups.

3. When choosing nibblies, no need to go to great expense. Start with your fridge and pantry. A mix of colours and shapes helps to make the platter look inviting. You can easily substitute cut up veggies and a healthy dip if you want a lighter nibble.

Present

A variety of nibblies allows your guest to graze at leisure, choosing what they will most enjoy.

Champagne with nibblies always goes well.

These types of nibbles can be served with pre-dinner drinks.

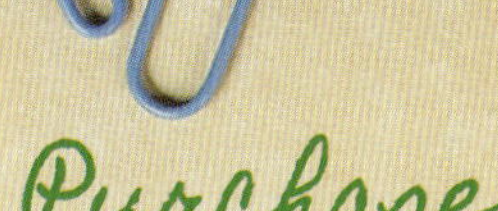

Purchase

FOR MIXED NIBBLES

200 gm thin sliced tasty salami

Variety of your favourite cheeses

Black olives

Sundried tomatoes

Gherkins

Strawberries

Parsley for decoration

Mixed crackers

STUFFED CAPSICUMS

Purchase:

1 pkt herb and garlic bread crumbs

2 eggs

Red and green capsicums

500 gm pork mince

½ cup parmesan cheese

½ cup chopped parsley

Baking paper

Prepare

1. In a mixing bowl, add mince, breadcrumbs, parmesan cheese, parsley and eggs, mixing well with your fingertips.

2. Cut the tops off the capsicums creating a lid.

3. Scoop out the seeds and the white lining from inside.

4. In a deep pot half filled with boiling water, add the capsicum bottoms and blanch until slightly soft.

5. Remove and allow to drip dry.

6. Stuff each capsicum with mix, making sure you press the mixture firmly into the capsicum.

7. Place lids back on each capsicum.

8. Place on a baking tray lined with baking paper.

9. Add a little water to the baking tray.

10. Place in a hot oven for 30 minutes or until the filling is cooked and the capsicum are browned.

11. Serve up on a warmed serving dish and garnish with parsley.

Present

It is usual for the skins of the capsicum lids to blacken a little. This is okay as the lids do not generally get eaten and it creates a visually pleasing effect.

When serving stuffed capsicums, place the lids askew, so that the content of the stuffed capsicum can be seen.

As an alternative stuffing, consider using cooked rice instead of bread crumbs, as this works well and adds texture to the finished dish.

You could also use yellow capsicum. I have chosen red and green to go with my colour theme.

Cutting a capsicum lengthwise to create boats also works well and you serve them flat.

Leave the stalks on the capsicum lids, as this allows you to more easily pick up the lid.

BERRY CREPES

Purchase:

1 tub mascarpone cheese

1 tub thickened cream

1 punnet strawberries

1 punnet blueberries

1 bottle passionfruit topping or similar

Icing sugar

1 pkt crepe stacks (pre-made)

Prepare

1. Place mascarpone and cream in a dish or bowl and mix well.
2. Separate the crepes and cover one side of the crepe with cream.
3. Slice strawberries and combine with berries and topping.
4. Spoon berry mix over crepes, concentrating it in the centre.
5. Gently roll the crepe and place on a plate.
6. Pour topping over the crepe and add a strawberry to the top as decoration with leaves on to add colour.
7. Generously dust with icing sugar.

Present

For the colder season, you may want to consider warming the crepes before adding the filling and serving up on a warm plate.

To ensure a great presentation, let the berries overflow the sides of the crepes, exposing the berries.

You could serve a dob of the mascarpone cheese on top or on the side of the plate or use icecream.

Choose the topping of your preference and the thicker the topping the better. You could easily use chocolate, caramel, strawberry, or even maple syrup.

RED SETTING

Prepare

Setting for four.

Place a white table cloth on the table.

Use the red serviettes as placemats, forming a cross shape and leaving a gap in the middle for the salt and pepper shakers and the vase.

Add the salt, pepper and vase with flowers to the table.

Place settings:

Place one square plate, one deep square bowl, knife, fork and spoon at each setting. I've chosen the green handled cutlery to give an Italian feel to the setting.

Add 1 tall wine glass.

Use the serviettes to create height and mix and match the red and white serviettes together.

Lay a large red serviette on the table. Add a smaller white one on top. Pinch in the centre and lift straight up, then rotate 180° and place in a water tumbler, creating the serviette shape in the picture.

Serve with a nice red wine.

Bread basket:

Place one red serviette in the bottom of a bread basket to match table setting and add sliced bread into the basket.

Or bread and butter plate:

Place the white doily on a square bread and butter plate, then sit the butter bowl on top, garnishing with parsley for a finishing touch. Place butter knife on the side.

Serve the crusty sliced Italian bread and butter on a cutting board, placed at the end of the table.

Purchase

White table cloth

9 large red serviettes
(one for the bread basket)

8 smaller white serviettes

4 tall wine glasses

4 short water tumblers

Cutlery

Salt and pepper shakers

Tall vase with single blossom flowers

5 square bread and butter plates
(one for the butter)

4 square bowls

Present

Put some soft instrumental music on in the background, as this is typically Italian.

This is a great setting for an Italian night or themed evening. I have asked my guests to dress in Italian style and surprise me. I have been treated to some beautiful green, red and white hats, Italian coloured clothing and one of my most unusual guests came wearing red and green shoes. One of my male guests, decked out immaculately in a lovely suit, assured me he was wearing Italian coloured undies.

CHORIZO SAUSAGE AND TURKISH BREAD

4 chorizo sausages

2 loaves Turkish bread

1 sprig parsley

Prepare

1. Cut chorizo sausage length ways into three or four slices.

2. Slice Turkish bread length ways and lightly toast in a hot oven for 2 mins.

3. Place chorizo sausage slices in a microwave safe cooking dish and cook on high for just under 1 minute.

4. Drain chorizo sausage on paper towel to absorb excess oil.

5. Place in a deep serving bowl on a serving tray. Arrange Turkish bread around the bowl and garnish with a little parsley.

6. Serve warm.

Cooking is one of the most fun activities to do. Not only will it bring a sense of achievement but it also unites a family.

Present

Cutting the sausage length ways allows the chorizo sausage to curl. It also keeps the sausage moist.

It's a great entrée to share with others. The spiciness of the sausage kick starts your appetite.

As a starter, serve with a nice liqueur. I've selected Galliano.

You can substitute any form of toasted bread instead of Turkish bread if you wish.

SPINACH & RICOTTA CANNELLONI

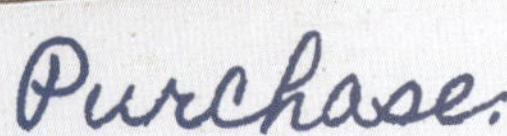

Purchase:

1 pkt fresh lasagne sheets

1 cup parmesan cheese

1 kilo fresh ricotta

1 bunch cooked spinach

4 eggs

500 gm tasty grated cheese

2 jars tomato cooking sauce

Salt and pepper

Olive oil

2 cups herb and garlic bread crumbs

1 cup water

Prepare

1. In a large bowl place ricotta, cooked spinach, ½ the parmesan cheese, and bread crumbs.

2. Add ½ grated cheese to the bowl.

3. Add 4 eggs.

4. Add salt and pepper and mix well.

5. Add your cooking sauce to a large oven proof glass dish.

6. Add one cup of water, using the water to clean the inside of the sauce jar, pouring over sauce.

7. Mix with a wooden spoon to evenly combine the sauce and the water and spread over the bottom of the dish.

8. Lay single sheets of lasagne pasta on your cutting board.

9. Spoon a generous portion of filling mixture onto each sheet at one end in preparation for rolling into cannelloni.

10. Firmly roll the lasagne sheet, keeping the ends open.

11. Fill the ends with extra mixture and place on top of sauce in the cooking dish.

12. Repeat until dish is filled (I have fit six cannelloni in my dish).

13. Pour the second jar of tomato cooking sauce on top of the cannelloni, covering completely.

14. Sprinkle with remaining parmesan and then add the grated cheese to cover the top.

15. Place a sheet of baking paper over the dish.

16. Seal with a sheet of alfoil.

17. Place glass dish on a baking tray and cook in a preheated oven at 180°C for 1 hour, removing alfoil and baking paper after 50 mins to brown the top.

18. Serve in the glass dish. Guests will serve themselves.

Present

For quick and easy preparation, frozen spinach works as well as fresh spinach.

It's a great meal for non-meat eating guests and can be classed as vegetarian.

By covering dish with baking paper and alfoil, you enable the cannelloni to cook quicker and still retain moisture.

Set cannelloni quite firmly together, as you will find that the pasta will expand when cooking.

Be generous with the filling as this will help you to roll the lasagne sheets.

Ensuring the top is well covered with sauce will keep the pasta soft, as it absorbs a lot of moisture.

The lasagne sheets are easier than filling a cannelloni shell and achieves the same effect.

Placing the glass dish on a baking tray, it makes it easier to manage in the oven.

Cooking in a nice glass dish helps with presentation as you are serving straight from the oven.

Cannelloni is perfect the next day as well and can be reheated in a microwave oven.

Cut the cannelloni in half to allow your guests to manage their portion sizes.

TIRAMASU

Purchase:

2 pkts Savoiardi biscuits
(sponge finger biscuits)

1 tub mascarpone cheese

1 punnet strawberries

1 Flake chocolate

500 gm thickened cream

½ cup instant coffee

½ cup sugar

½ cup icing sugar, plus extra for dusting

2 cups hot water

Chocolate dipping sauce sachet
(or chocolate topping)

Prepare

1. In a large container, place sugar and coffee.

2. Dissolve with hot water and mix well with an egg whisk.

3. In a separate bowl, mix cream and mascarpone cheese together.

4. Add ½ cup of icing sugar to the cream and mascarpone cheese.

5. Mix well.

6. Dip the sponge fingers into the coffee syrup and place in deep glass dish. Repeat the process, forming a row of soggy sponge fingers. Fill the bottom of the dish.

7. Generously spread the cream mix over the top of the sponge fingers and add another layer of soggy sponge fingers.

8. Cover with the remaining cream mix, ensuring all the sponge fingers are covered.

9. With a fork, make swirly patterns in the cream.

10. Crumble the Flake into little flakes and sprinkle on top of the cream.

11. Cut strawberries in half, leaving green tips on.

12. Place strawberries in rows evenly over the top.

13. Creatively drizzle chocolate sauce on top of tiramasu.

14. Dust with icing sugar and refrigerate.

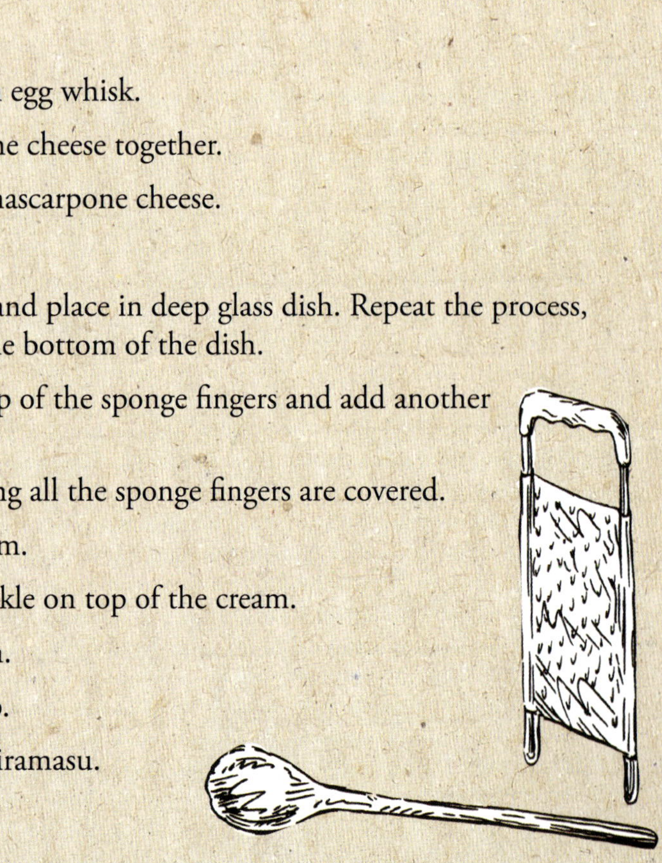

Present

The perfect dessert to prepare a day in advance.

You can use hot chocolate or milo instead of coffee.

For those that like a stronger taste, you can add Tia Maria or another liqueur to the coffee mixture.

A great dessert for a smorgasbord.

You can also create individual serves using parfait glasses. Stand the soaked sponge fingers upright in each glass. Fill with cream and garnish each glass with a full flake, a strawberry and a swirl of dipping chocolate.

If you do not have access to Savoiardi biscuits, you can substitute with Nice biscuits or any plain sweet biscuits. Just add double the biscuit portion to the recipe.

As an experiment, I tried using ginger nut biscuits generously soaked in the coffee mixture and left them in the fridge for two days to allow them to soften. It really was a taste sensation.

By using thickened cream you don't have to whip the cream and mascarpone cheese saving you time and energy.

Of all my desserts, tiramasu receives the most positive comments…everyone wants Grace's tiramasu.

VINTAGE
FALLS
CLASSIC DRY RED

ORIENTAL SETTING

Purchase

1 floral table cloth with an oriental influence

Wooden salt and pepper shakers

Cutlery for two settings – 2 knives, 4 forks, 2 dessert spoons

2 oriental style serving spoons

2 red cocktail glasses or similar

4 large red serviettes

2 white cups

2 square white saucers

2 white serving dishes on black trays

1 long rectangular serving tray

1 sushi spoon tray, with six matching spoons

2 black wine goblets

1 bottle red wine

1 white square dipping sauce bowl

1 glass serving tray

2 square bread and butter plates

2 deep square white dishes

Present

Place oriental table cloth on the table.

Create two settings by placing one black tray, with the white serving dish on top. Then add a folded serviette with one of the oriental serving spoons on top next to the tray, placing the other cutlery alongside.

Place the cup and saucer and cocktail glass above the serviette on the right of the setting.

Serve food in the middle of the table.

Place your bottle of red wine on the table and strategically place your salt and pepper shakers.

Tips

When presenting Sushi, cut into rounds and leave larger portions in the centre to create some height and variation.

By creating your own variations of food on individual serving spoons, you offer the opportunity for guests to try different combinations.

Sushi is a great starter and can be served with pre dinner drinks.

I have had some fun with wasabi, but it should be used with caution. Although hot cheeks and panting can be seen as funny, it's not so amusing for the guest.

When combining oriental foods, complement spicy flavours with a palate cleanser, like rockmelon for example.

Oriental foods lend themselves to a self-service model of entertaining and are great in winter because they warm you on the inside.

SUSHI ROLLS

Purchase:

**Utilise what you already have.
I have chosen to use:**

Cracked green olives

Semi sundried tomatoes

Tasty Blue Vein cheese

Sushi roll

Parsley

Prepare

1. For convenience, frozen high quality sushi rolls are readily available from your local supermarket. Choosing pre-prepared sushi ensures that you get consistently high quality of presentation and taste every time.

2. I keep sushi in my freezer as a quick standby for unexpected guests. It thaws out quickly, tastes fresh and I can slice it as needed.

3. Serve with soy sauce in a dipping dish.

4. Place bite sized portions on each spoon. You can mix and match the foods.

5. Serve on a tray, garnished with parsley.

Present

Seafood would be a great alternative, i.e. scallops, prawns etc served with a wedge of lemon.

You can pick up a set of oriental spoons and bowls very cheaply from your local oriental supermarket.

I believe our children should be taught to cook and entertain. Theses skills are a true investment for life.

SWEET AND SOUR MEAT BALLS AND RICE

Purchase

1 kg Swedish meatballs

1 jar sweet and sour sauce

1 large cup rice

1 sprig parsley

1 tbsp salt

Prepare

1. Put a pot of hot water on to boil.

2. Add 1 tablespoon of salt to the water.

3. Add 1 cup of rice to the boiling water. Cook for 12 mins, checking regularly to make sure it doesn't boil dry.

4. Line a baking tray with baking paper.

5. Place meat balls on the baking paper.

6. Place in a preheated hot oven and cook at 180°C for 10 mins.

7. Remove the meatballs from the oven.

8. Strain the rice and place in a large serving bowl.

9. Place the bowl in the centre of a deep serving plate.

10. Arrange the meatballs around the rice bowl.

11. Pour sauce into a microwave safe bowl.

12. Heat in the microwave for 1 min.

13. Pour the sweet and sour sauce over the meatballs.

14. Garnish rice with a sprig of parsley.

15. Serve as a centrepiece for self-serving.

Present

I choose to use these meatballs because I discovered they were equally as good as my own creations and way more convenient.

This whole main meal can be prepared in less than 20 minutes.

You can also serve individually in warmed ramekins, with warmed rice in the bottom and meatballs on top.

CARAMELISED PEACHES WITH MASCARPONE

Purchase:

8 firm free stone peaches

1 tub mascarpone cheese

2 cups sugar

1 cup water

Icing sugar for dusting

Chocolate dipping sauce

Handful of strawberries

Prepare

1. Cut the peaches in half and remove the stone.

2. In a glass baking dish lined with baking paper, place the peach halves face up until the dish is full.

3. Sprinkle sugar evenly over the peaches.

4. Pour cold water over the peaches.

5. Place tray in a pre-heated oven (180°C) and cook for 10 mins only.

6. Remove peaches from the oven.

7. Place the peaches face up in a deep serving dish.

8. Spoon liquid from the baking dish over the peaches.

9. Scoop a teaspoon of mascarpone cheese into the centre of each peach.

10. Dust generously with icing sugar.

Present

This recipe can be used for apricots, plums and most stone fruits.

The fruit must be firm for best effect.

Very important not to overcook.

Can also be served with ice cream or whipped cream.

Great with a latte or cappuccino or strong short black.

Variation: Individual Serves

On a large white plate, drizzle ice magic chocolate, creating a pattern.

Place three peach halves into the middle of the plate.

Scoop a teaspoon of mascarpone into the centre of each peach.

Cut strawberries into halves and place decoratively on the side of the plate and dust with icing sugar.

Serve while warm.

COLOURFUL SETTING

Plan

Setting for two.

Place green placemats at each setting.

Add colourful paper placemat on top.

Place one large green serviette on the table and then place a white smaller serviette in the centre. Pinch in the middle and flip 180° and place in water tumbler as per presentation in photo.

Add cutlery to the setting.

Place bread and butter plates on the side.

Add one tall wine glass to the setting.

Place patterned plate in the centre and add salt and pepper shakers and butter dish on opposite sides.

Purchase

2 colourful paper placemats

2 green material placemats

2 tall wine glasses

2 long water tumblers

2 large green serviettes

2 small white serviettes

Salt and Pepper shakers

Cutlery

2 double-sided bread and butter plates

1 butter dish with lid and butter knife

1 patterned centre plate for serving

Present

By using the proper placemat under the colourful paper placemat you are adding cushioning to the setting which will cut down noise and protects the table. It also adds substance to the setting.

By not using a full tablecloth allows the wood of the table top to be seen, adding warmth to the setting.

Perfect for a light lunch with a girlfriend.

A simple table setting can be effective without costing the earth.

Serve with a nice light white wine or a bottle of bubbly.

SALMON

Purchase:

2 salmon fillets

1 lemon

1 sprig parsley

1 cup butter

1 pkt Roasted Garlic & Herbs
Finishing Sauce

Baby spinach for green salad

Paprika for sprinkling

1 tomato

Prepare

1. Season salmon fillets with salt and pepper.

2. Add butter to a frying pan and heat.

3. When butter is sizzling, add salmon fillets to the frying pan and cook on high heat for 3 mins each side, adding extra salt and pepper when you turn them over. Salmon should be golden brown when cooked properly.

4. While the salmon is cooking, prepare a bed of baby spinach in deep serving dishes.

5. Thinly slice lemon rounds.

6. Serve salmon on top of the bed of baby spinach.

7. Add rounds of lemon to the plate.

8. Heat the finishing sauce in the microwave in a microwave proof jug.

9. Pour over cooked salmon.

10. Sprinkle paprika over the salmon.

11. Slice the tomato and place one slice on top of the salmon.

Present

Sprinkle extra paprika around the edge of the plate to give a restaurant finish. Looks fabulous on white plates.

It is important to not overcook the salmon.

Thicker portions take a little longer to cook through.

To ensure that the salmon is fully cooked insert a skewer through the thickest part of the fillet. If the skewer comes out easily, the salmon is cooked.

Salmon is the perfect entrée and high in Omega 3.

A great healthy start to your luncheon.

Roasted Garlic
& Herbs
Finishing Sauce

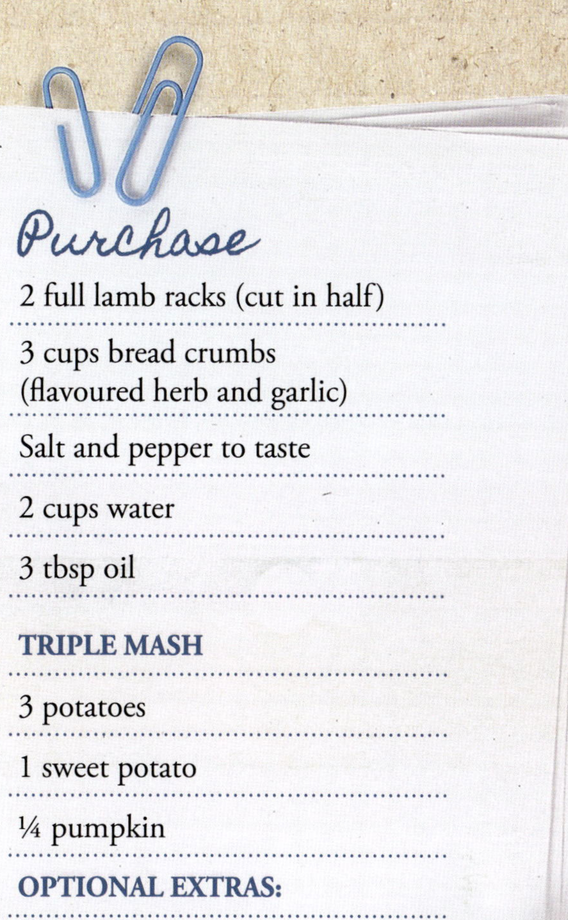

Purchase

2 full lamb racks (cut in half)

3 cups bread crumbs
(flavoured herb and garlic)

Salt and pepper to taste

2 cups water

3 tbsp oil

TRIPLE MASH

3 potatoes

1 sweet potato

¼ pumpkin

OPTIONAL EXTRAS:

Dob of butter

Mild mustard

Prepare

1. Pour water into a baking dish lined with paper.

2. Roll lamb in bread crumbs, pressing firmly and place into baking dish.

3. Drizzle oil and season with salt and pepper. Sprinkle extra crumbs onto lamb.

4. Cover with baking paper and then foil. Cook in a hot oven at 180°C for 1 hour.

5. Turn off heat and you can either rest the lamb in the oven or on the bench.

6. Steam, boil or microwave vegetables, then in a bowl mash with a little milk, salt and pepper. Add butter and mustard to taste.

7. Serve lamb on scoops of triple mash and decorate with a paper frill and a sprig of rosemary.

Present

A great local red wine will finish off this part of the meal nicely.

Adding water and covering the dish ensures that the lamb remains moist and tender.

Works really well with a side dish of steamed stringless beans served wrapped in proscuitto or steamed asparagus in a light butter sauce.

Paper Frills

To make paper frills, cut a sheet of A4 paper in half to create an A5 size. Fold the A5 sheet in half length ways. Cut thin slits along the folded edge (cut 2/3 of the way through, making sure not to cut all the way through). Cut the strip in half to create two frills. Turn the folded paper inside out (this makes the frills puff out like a hat) and wrap around to form a small circle, securing with some sticky tape.

Place the frill over the end of the bone on the lamb rack.

You can make frills up in advance in your spare time and keep them in the cupboard.

STRAWBERRY & CHOCOLATE DELIGHT

Purchase

1 punnet strawberries

2 tbsp mascarpone cheese

Chocolate dipping sauce

Prepare

1. Wash and freeze strawberries, keeping the leaves on.
2. Drizzle chocolate in the bottom of long white parfait glasses and fill to the top with frozen strawberries.
3. Pour chocolate generously over the strawberries and top with a spoon full of mascarpone and half a strawberry.

Present

The chocolate will set over the frozen strawberries, creating a crunchy chocolate covering. This results in a unique texture and flavour that is quite refreshing.

To enjoy this dessert any time of the year, buy strawberries when they are in season and freeze them.

You may prepare this dessert before guests arrive, but it should be stored in the fridge so that it is chilled and the strawberries are slightly thawed.

To enhance the flavour of strawberries, add a splash of balsamic vinegar.

FAMILY FILLERS

Being from a large European family who came through difficult times, I learned a lot about creating meals in large volume by observing my mother. I was always amazed at how she could produce meals from the simplest of ingredients, mostly taken from our own garden. Mum used to cook meals all in one pot - she called them one-pot-meals - which was great at the time because it meant not too much washing up!

Even though we never had a lot of variety nor fancy foods, I remember Mum always had a pot of food ready and we never went hungry. I learned a lot of my cooking skills from Mum and the older women that surrounded my life. I guess that is why I always cook in volume, just in case unexpected visitors come along or war breaks out and we might go hungry... You can never be too sure what calamity faces us. In my view a well stocked pantry is a definite advantage.

My guests are always grateful for the bags of goodies they leave my table with and it gives me great pleasure to be able to share in abundance what I have been blessed with.

To me 'family fillers' are meals that can be put together with a minimum of fuss from ingredients that are readily available in your pantry. They are dishes that are tasty, satisfying and loosely guided by a recipe. Open the door for your individual creativity. I encourage you to experiment and find the flavours that suit your family best. Enjoy being able to warmly welcome extra mouths at your table with these lovely family fillers.

When you bulk cook, it gives you the opportunity to package and freeze meals, perfect for unplanned events.

Be adventurous. Discovering your favourite foods that combine well to make a dish can be very satisfying and at the end of the day you hold the bragging rights!

When my children kept nagging me about what's for dinner, I always told them we're having YMCA. "Yesterday's meal cooked again!"

Purchase

1 pkt 500 gm pasta spirals or penne

1 whole cooked chicken

1 cup sun dried tomatoes (semi dried)

½ cup fresh parsley – chopped finely

500ml cream

1 cup tasty cheese – shredded

½ cup parmesan cheese

8 savoury crackers

Prepare

1. Bring large pot of salted water to the boil and add pasta. Boil pasta, drain and cool.

2. Fleece cooked chicken – removing bones and skin.

3. In a deep casserole or baking dish, place cooked pasta.

4. Cover the pasta with the fleeced, cooked chicken meat.

5. On top of the chicken spread the sun dried tomatoes and shredded cheese.

6. Pour cream evenly over the top and then sprinkle with chopped parsley.

7. Roughly crumble crackers and spread over the entire dish.

8. With a sheet of baking paper, gently but firmly press all the ingredients down, neatly pressing the edges.

9. Remove paper. Sprinkle the dish with parmesan cheese.

10. Bake in hot oven 180°C for 35mins.

11. Serve warm or cold with a green salad.

Present

Colour is very important in this dish. I have chosen sundried tomatoes because of their vivid colouring and their zingy flavour.

Presenting this dish straight from the oven to the table works well for a serve yourself meal.

For ease of cutting, let the pasta stand for a while after it is cooked. This meal will stretch to feed a large number of guests and can be cooked prior to guests arrival.

RABBIT CASSEROLE

Purchase

1 whole farm or wild rabbit

6 small whole potatoes

1 lrg onion

Fresh parsley

1 clove garlic

1 jar tomato cooking sauce

Salt and pepper to flavour

1 pkt ready prepared polenta square

Prepare

1. Portion the rabbit into approximately 8 pieces.

2. Place in a saucepan filled with a little salted water and bring to the boil.

3. Let the rabbit boil for 5 mins. Remove and wash the rabbit under cold running water. (See present section for reason why.)

4. In a deep pan, fry onion and garlic in a little oil.

5. Add rabbit and cook until brown.

6. Pour in tomato cooking sauce and then fill up the jar with water, shake and pour into the pan.

7. Add salt and pepper.

8. Cover and let simmer for 1 hour.

9. Peel potatoes and add to the rabbit.

10. Simmer until the potatoes are cooked and the rabbit is tender. Chop the fresh parsley and fold through the casserole.

11. Warm the prepared polenta square in the microwave. Cut into strips.

12. Pour the rabbit casserole into a metal warming dish (with candles underneath) and serve with sliced polenta in a separate dish.

13. Serve with crusty Italian bread and a glass of home made wine.

Present

Boiling and washing the rabbit removes the game flavour and speeds up the cooking time.

Home made polenta works just as well as pre-packaged. If you prefer, you can substitute polenta with home made dumplings, mashed potatoes, or a green salad.

For a European flavour, add a few black olives, a touch of chilli and a bowl of fresh fennel. Fennel is fabulous for refreshing the palate.

For tenderising your red meat, add red wine to game meats, such as, rabbit, venison, duck and quail.

MINCE PIES

Purchase

- 1 kg beef mince
- 1 lrg chopped onion
- 1 pkt frozen mixed veggies
- 1 pkt ready roll puff pastry
- 1 egg lightly beaten
- ½ cup tasty shredded cheese
- 2 cups stock – beef or vegetable
- Salt and pepper to taste

Prepare

1. In a large saucepan or deep fry pan, heat a little oil and the chopped onions. When the onions are soft (appear clear), add the mince and cook til brown.

2. Add stock to the pan and cook for 15 mins.

3. Add vegetables and cook for a further 10 mins, until vegetables are tender.

4. Add salt and pepper to taste.

Individual Pies

1. To make individual pies, spoon the mixture into ramekins and set aside.

2. Cover each ramekin with ½ a sheet of thawed puff pastry. (See picture)

3. Cut off excess pastry with a sharp knife by following the edge of the dish. Use the excess pastry to form a small scroll, rose or centrepiece. You can be creative.

4. Glaze pastry with a lightly beaten egg.

5. Place ramekins on a baking tray and cook in a hot oven for 25 mins or until pastry is golden brown.

Family Pie

1. Spray the deep baking tray with cooking oil.

2. Line the bottom of the tray with puff pastry, overlapping the sides.

3. Pour the meat mixture on top of the pastry and fill the tray.

4. Spread evenly and press firmly with a spoon.

5. Sprinkle with a little grated tasty cheese for that little bit of extra flavour and then cover top with puff pastry.

6. Fold over the edges, sealing the top and pinching the sides together.

7. Take out another sheet of thawed puff pastry and cut into long, thin strips.

8. Crisscross the strips on top of the pie to create a woven effect.

9. Add a little ball of pastry in the centre of the pie.

10. Generously glaze the top with a lightly beaten egg.

11. Place in a hot oven and cook for 45 mins or until pastry is golden brown and crisp.

Present

Remember, pies don't take long to cook because the meat is already cooked. The most important part of a successful pie, is the crisp and golden pastry.

I love using puff pastry; the ready rolled variety. This works well for me and is one of my quick and easy supplies I have on hand for the unexpected meal.

I love serving this pie as a family entertainer. As a main meal, I present individual pies with a delicious home made gravy and a side salad.

You can change the meat to suit your personal tastes. Pork, steak or chicken work well using the same method.

GRACE'S SENSATIONAL FETTUCCINI PASTA BAKE

Purchase

1 pkt green fettuccini pasta

1 pkt white fettuccini pasta

Spray on oil

1 tub fresh ricotta

1 pkt fresh baby spinach leaves

6 eggs lightly beaten

4 sliced ripe tomatoes

2 cups grated cheese

250 gm diced bacon

1 cup chopped spring onion

Prepare

1. In a large deep pot, bring water to the boil.

2. Add a little salt to the water.

3. When the water is rapidly boiling, add fettuccini pasta and cook until al dente (soft but not mushy), approximately 10-15 mins.

4. Remove pasta from the water and drain. Set aside to cool.

5. In a deep glass casserole dish, spray a little oil and lay the pasta in the dish.

6. Spread ricotta evenly over the pasta.

7. Top with fresh spinach leaves.

8. Pour the beaten eggs over the top.

9. Layer sliced tomatoes over the top of the spinach.

10. Combine bacon, cheese and spring onions in a bowl. Sprinkle the mixture over the top of the tomatoes.

11. Place in a hot oven, 180°C, for 20 mins.

12. Cut into portions and serve on a warm plate, with a side serve of fresh spinach.

Present

Using two different coloured fettuccini gives the finished dish an added visual effect.

Very important that you do not overcook the pasta, as it continues cooking when you put it back into the oven.

Allowing the dish to stand a little before you serve makes it easier to cut and serve, as the egg sets.

This also works well cold.

Reheat leftovers in the microwave.

This is a low budget, high impact meal and can easily double as a vegetarian dish by removing the bacon.

This dish can also be prepared with other forms of pasta…for example, penne, spiral, bow or macaroni.

SAVOURY HAM AND EGG MUFFINS

Purchase

24 slices round ham

500 gm diced bacon

3 cups diced spring onions

1½ dozen eggs

2 cups tasty shredded cheese

Prepare

1. Generously spray a large 12 hole muffin tray with cooking oil.

2. Stack the ham and slit to enable each slice to sit into the muffin tray.

3. Line each muffin hole with two slices of ham, using the slit to cross over the edges to form a shell.

4. In a bowl, combine the spring onions, cheese, and bacon. In a separate bowl beat six eggs. Add the egg mixture to the combined ingredients and mix well. (To minimise cleaning you could easily prepare the eggs first and then add the dry ingredients to the egg mixture).

5. Spoon mixture into each of the ham muffin shells. Don't over fill. Leave room for an egg.

6. Gently break one whole egg into each muffin.

7. Place the muffin tray into a hot oven and cook for 25 mins or until the eggs are coagulated and the ham is crisp.

Present

This is a great breakfast dish and good for catering for larger numbers as everyone is getting a whole meal in each serve.

For those who find it hard to eat whole eggs (ie can't eat coagulated egg yolks or white), simply break the yoke and mix the egg white and yoke together and pour in.

To save time in preparation, cut the ham all in one go by creating a stack.

This is great served up on a nice black serving dish with a sprig of parsley or you can serve with warm toast and sliced tomato.

To be a successful cook you must be organised, tidy and think ahead.

Hayley's MOUTH WATERING TURKEY

Purchase

1 boneless pre-cooked turkey breast

1 jar cranberry jam or sauce

Prepare

Score the top of the turkey breast in a crisscross pattern.

Generously glaze with cranberry sauce or jam using a pastry brush.

Bake in a hot oven for 15 mins, until the jam caramelises.

Serve on a hot plate and carve at the table.

Present

This turkey is delish cold or hot. If you serve it cold, serve with salad or home made coleslaw. If your serve it hot, serve with cauliflower and cheese, steamed peas, beans or asparagus.

My friend, Hayley, loves turkey and I wanted to show her how quick and easy it is to create a mouth-watering turkey meal that takes less than 30 mins to prepare. She was delighted.

Turkey is a great way for you to enjoy Christmas in July and December, as it is available throughout the year. My friend, Hayley, says, "It doesn't have to be Christmas to have a turkey, cause' it's Christmas at Grace's every day."

Always thaw frozen meat in a refrigerator so bacteria cannot grow.

RECIPE
MARINATED PORK RIBS

Purchase

4 sheets fresh pork ribs

2 jars honey soy marinade

2 cups water

Salt and pepper

Prepare

1. Line a deep baking tray with baking paper.

2. Lay the pork ribs on the tray and sprinkle with a little bit of salt.

3. Cover the ribs with honey soy marinade.

4. Pour the 2 cups of water into the tray.

5. Cover with baking paper.

6. Overlay with foil so it makes a tight, sealed lid. This makes the ribs cook in their own juices.

7. Heat oven to 180°C and bake for 2 hours. Steam cook until tender.

8. Let ribs cool for 15 mins before serving.

9. These ribs are delicious served as an entrée or as individual serves of one sheet per person for a main meal.

Present

When presenting, use a large white glass platter to contrast the colour of the ribs.

Sprinkle a few sesame seeds to give it that professional finish.

Add a sprig of parsley for a splash of colour.

This makes a beautiful shared entrée and is a fun family meal.

I'm sure you will agree there is nothing like the feel of a warm damp hand towel heated in the microwave for a few seconds…reminds me of flying.

This recipe is my absolute favourite and a winner with all of my guests!

Purchase

1 leg of lamb on the bone

Sprigs rosemary

Garlic cloves

Salt and pepper to taste

Olive oil

1 cup water

Prepare

1. With a sharp boning knife, remove the bone from the leg of lamb by running the knife down the side of the bone, and push the sides apart to enable you to cut the bone out, whilst keeping the meat in one piece.

2. Remove the meat from the shank bone (see picture).

3. Start to butterfly the meat (cutting layers off the top of the thick portions but leaving them attached, opening them out like a butterfly's wings). The goal is to create one piece of meat with it all the same thickness. Continue this process until the meat is even all over. This will enable the meat to cook evenly (see picture).

4. Trim off any excess fat.

5. Line a baking dish with baking paper and add the meat distributing evenly over the bottom of the pan.

6. Generously sprinkle salt and pepper to taste.

7. Roughly chop garlic cloves and spread over the meat.

8. Add sprigs of rosemary to the top of the meat in the pan.

9. Pour 1 cup of water over the meat.

10. Drizzle a little olive oil on top.

11. Cover the baking dish with baking paper.

12. Place a sheet of foil over the top and cook in a hot oven on 180°C.

13. Cook for 2 hours.

14. Remove foil and let the lamb stand for 15-20 mins.

15. Juices from the pan will make a gravy.

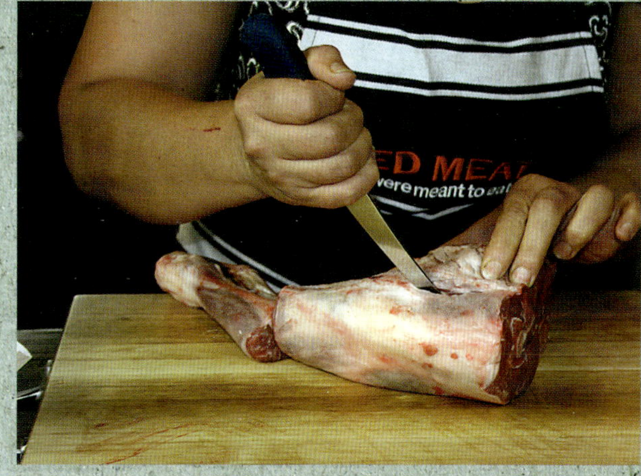

continued >

Present

For best presentation and results, I recommend that the lamb is light pink in colour. Be careful not to overcook it, as this tends to dry out the meat.

Covering the lamb enables the meat to cook in it's own juices, guaranteeing that it is tender and moist.

Removing the bone makes carving the meat much easier and less time consuming.

You can achieve the same results by using the same method and leaving the bone in. However, remember that meat cooked with the bone in cooks quicker, so reduce the cooking time by approx 15 mins.

Always remember, you must carve against the grain for best presentation.

I like to slice lamb and leave it in the pan juices until I am ready to serve as this stops the meat from drying out.

Perfect with roasted root vegetables or if you want to have a cold meal, home made pickles and a tossed green salad or crusty rolls. Or for that good old Aussie finish, you can whack on some tomato sauce.

SEMI-BONELESS CHICKEN ROAST

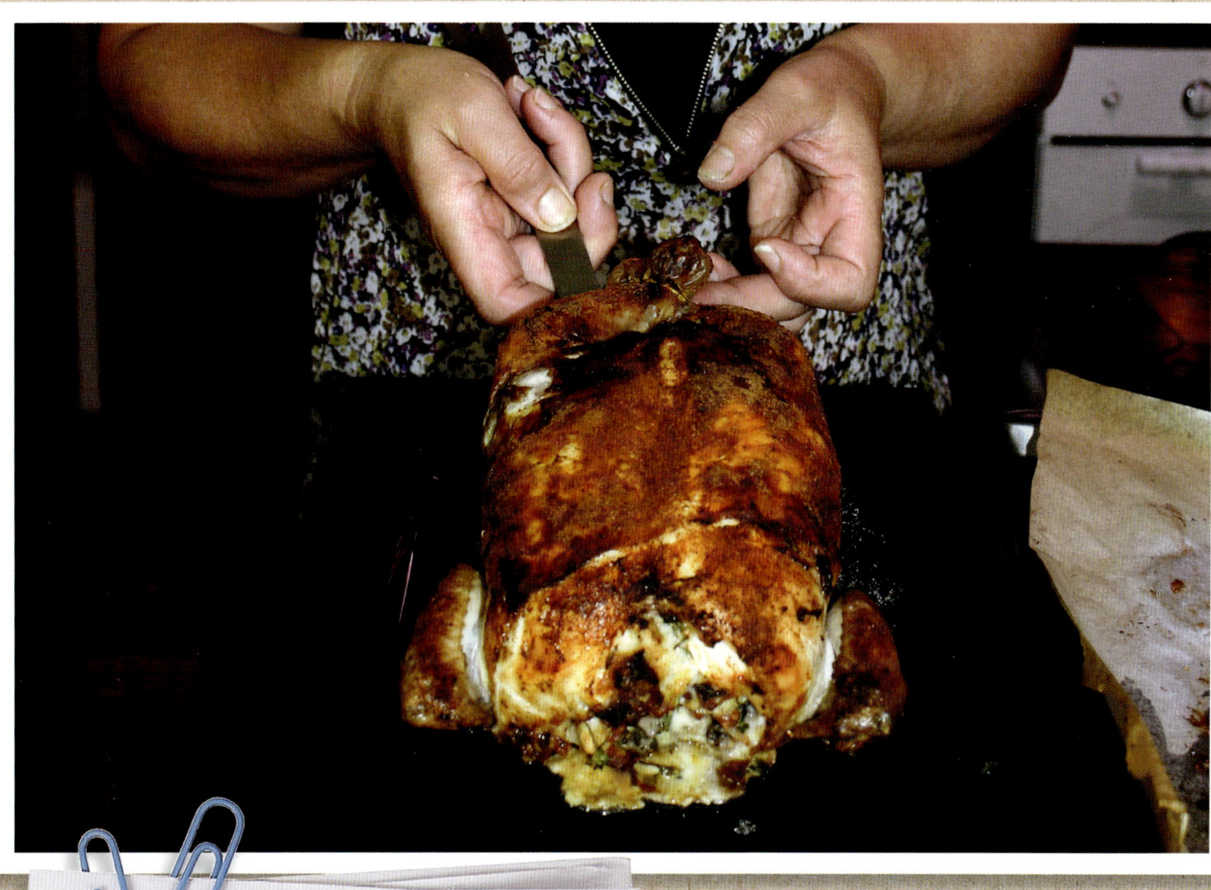

Purchase

1 whole lrg chicken

2 eggs

½ cup fresh parsley

Paprika

Tooth picks

250 gm diced bacon or diced ham

4 slices wholemeal bread

2 chicken loops or string

1 cup tasty shredded cheese

Salt and pepper to taste

Prepare

1. Prepare a stuffing by adding the diced bacon or ham to a deep bowl. Crumble and add the bread.
2. Roughly chop the parsley and add to bowl.
3. Break two eggs over the bowl.
4. Add cheese, salt and pepper and using your clean fingers, combine all ingredients and set aside.

continued >

SEMI-BONELESS CHICKEN ROAST
(CONTINUED)

Prepare

BONING THE CHICKEN

1. Place chicken on it's tummy and with a sharp boning knife, slit the backbone of the chicken on either side following down to the breast bone.

2. Keeping the knife as close to the bone as possible, gently remove the bone, making sure that the chicken is still in one piece (see picture).

3. Remove the carcass from the chicken.

4. Remove the thigh bone, keeping the drumsticks still intact and attached to the chicken.

5. Remove the breast bone.

6. Place handfuls of stuffing mix in the centre of the chicken, pressing firmly into the meat.

7. Pull the edges of the skin together, securing with toothpicks.

8. Turn the chicken on it's back and flip the wings under the chicken.

9. Loop the legs together and generously sprinkle paprika over the top.

10. Place on a baking tray lined with baking paper and cook in a hot oven 180°C for 1¾ hours.

11. Remove from the oven and let stand on a platter until ready to carve and serve.

12. For easy serving, carve the chicken by cutting the wings and replacing them, then the drumsticks and then slicing through the breast. Should be served on a warm plate with all pieces back in place.

13. This is an easy carve chicken. Use a sharp steak knife and by having removed the bones, you will get a great result, with the stuffing displayed beautifully.

Present

Add a sprig of parsley to add a splash of colour.

This is a delightful centrepiece and it doesn't have to be Christmas to enjoy this meal. Guests will love it!

After removing the bones from the chicken, keep them to create stock by boiling them in water.

For the stuffing, day old bread works best.

To tenderise your chicken soak or marinate in a little buttermilk.

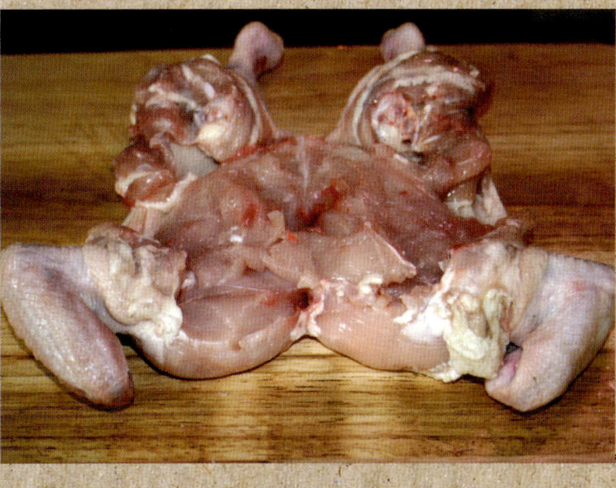

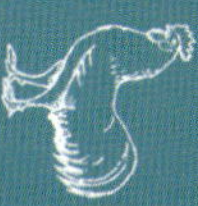

GRACE'S QUICK AND EASY CHICKEN LASAGNE

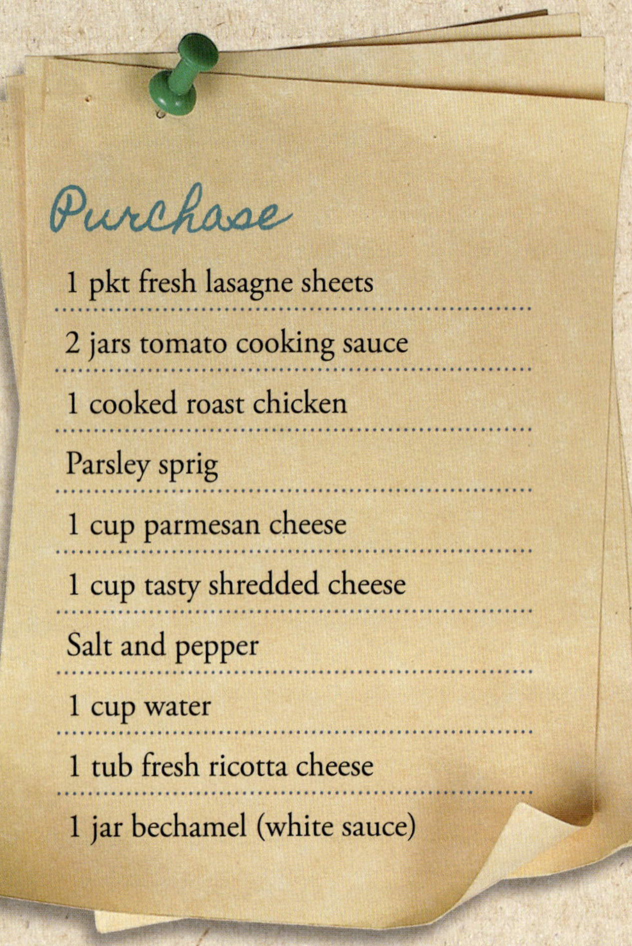

Purchase

1 pkt fresh lasagne sheets

2 jars tomato cooking sauce

1 cooked roast chicken

Parsley sprig

1 cup parmesan cheese

1 cup tasty shredded cheese

Salt and pepper

1 cup water

1 tub fresh ricotta cheese

1 jar bechamel (white sauce)

Prepare

1. Fleece the chicken, removing skin and bone and shred into thin pieces.

2. Pour a cup of water into an oven dish - square casserole or glass dish.

3. Lay sheets of lasagne to cover the base of the dish.

4. Spoon tomato cooking sauce generously over the lasagne.

5. Sprinkle shredded chicken over the sauce, along with a little parmesan, ricotta and cheese.

6. Place another sheet of lasagne on the top and repeat this method until all ingredients are used. Then finish with cheese.

7. Pour the béchamel sauce on top and sprinkle with a little cheese.

8. Cover with a sheet of baking paper and then a layer of foil.

9. Seal the edges and place in a pre-heated oven and cook for 1 hour at 180°C.

10. When cooked, remove the paper. Place the tray back in the oven and brown the top.

Present

Covering the lasagne with baking paper and foil, retains all the moisture, cooks quicker and guarantees that the pasta is soft and tender. It also prevents the pasta from drying out and the ends burning.

I choose to use baking paper between the food and the foil because foil is made from aluminium, so I am keen to keep it separated. It also means that the food doesn't stick to the aluminium, which makes it hard for you to present the food well.

When cooking lasagne, you must let it stand for at least 30 mins before serving. Pasta keeps cooking while it is standing. If you wait, it will firm up and make it easier for you to cut and serve.

Lasagna is perfect cooked the day before, then refrigerated and reheated, as it is easier to cut.

When I use jars of sauce I often use a little water to clean the inside of the jar and add a little extra moisture to my dish. This dish is perfect for this purpose.

GRACE'S QUICK AND EASY CHICKEN LASAGNE

grace's

Purchase

250 gm short cut or eye bacon rashers

1 lrg onion

1 garlic clove

Parsley sprigs

6 small ripe tomatoes

1 lamb's fry (whole, light in colour)

1pkt haloumi cheese

½ cup flour

Salt and pepper to taste.

½ cup butter

Prepare

1. Remove skin from Lamb's fry as pictured.

2. Slice into thin strips.

3. Place flour and salt and pepper in a plastic bag for coating.

4. Add lambs fry to the plastic bag and twist off the end. Jiggle the bag around until all the lambs fry is coated in flour.

5. Add butter to a hot, deep frying pan (either electric or stove top).

6. Add coated lambs fry to the hot pan.

7. Gently cook both sides on moderate heat, making sure you don't over cook.   Turn the frying pan off and slice the onion and bacon into strips.

8. Slice the tomatoes.

9. Push the lambs fry to one side of the pan, and throw in the bacon, onion and tomato.

10. Turn the heat back on and cook until tender.

11. Combine the lambs fry, onion, tomato and bacon, and remove from the heat.

12. Slice the haloumi cheese into strips.

13. In a separate non-stick frying pan, gently cook the strips of haloumi until golden brown.

Present

In a deep serving dish, present lambs fry, bacon, tomatoes and onions.

On a separate serving tray present haloumi cheese and complement with sliced bread or dinner roles and garnish with a sprig of parsley for a splash of colour.

Haloumi cheese needs to be served immediately for best results.

My lambs fry and bacon tastes better reheated the next day.

This makes a beautiful winter dish or an ideal breakfast for the hearty man in your life.

Some people like to add gravy or tomato sauce, but I find that there is enough liquid or natural juices from the tomatoes, onions and meats to not need anything else.

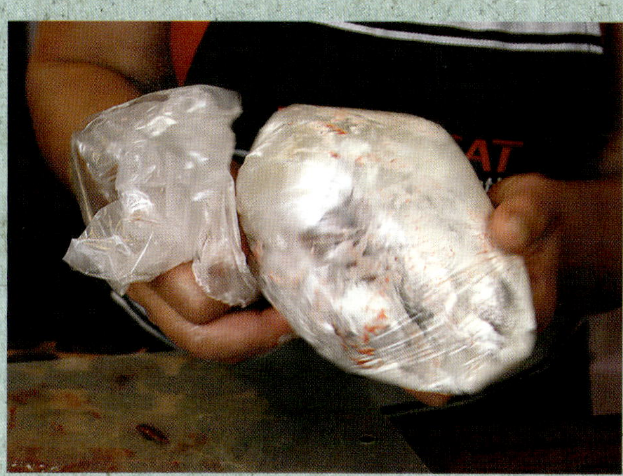
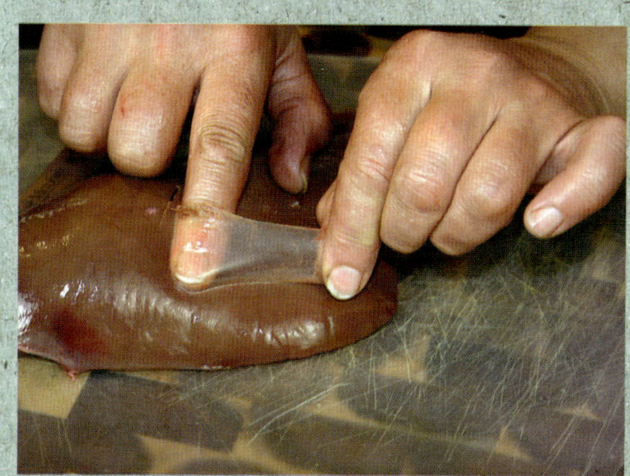

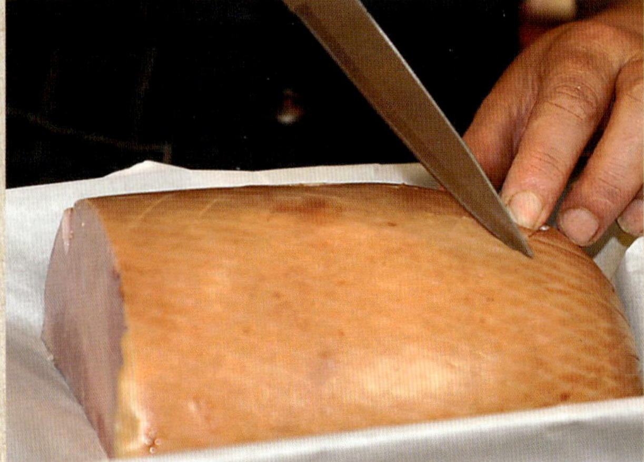

Purchase

1 lrg portion leg ham
(either on or off the bone)

1 jar orange or lemon
marmalade jam

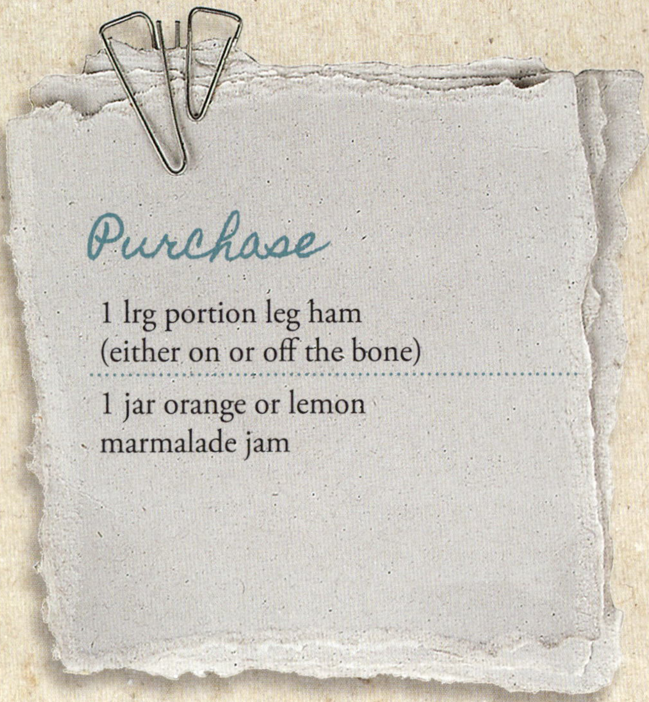

Prepare

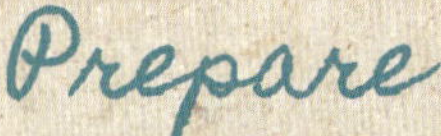

1. Cut the top of the ham in a crisscross pattern.

2. Generously glaze with marmalade.

3. Place on grease proof paper in a deep oven tray.

4. Place in hot oven 200°C and cook for 15-20 mins until the marmalade has caramelised and the outside is crispy.

5. Remove from oven and serve hot or cold.

Present

Serve on a large glass platter and carve as required.

It doesn't have to be Christmas to enjoy a lovely glazed ham.

Add a sprig of parsley for some additional colour.

For such easy preparation this dish has a huge impact on guests.

This is a quick addition to your menu and a winner when you want to 'ham it up' as ham is readily available.

BREAD AND BUTTER PUDDING

Purchase

1 loaf fruit bread

6 eggs

250 ml thickened cream

1 cup milk

½ cup sugar

1 tbsp vanilla essence

1 ltr milk

Icing sugar for dusting

1 punnet strawberries

1 bottle chocolate sauce

Cinnamon or nutmeg to flavour

Prepare

1. Taking one slice at a time, dip the fruit bread into a bowl of milk until it is soft and then place in a deep baking dish, layering until all the bread is used.

2. Put eggs, milk, cream, sugar and vanilla essence in a mixing bowl and mix well with a fork.

3. When all ingredients are combined, pour over the soaked bread in the baking tray, pushing the bread down firmly so that all the mixture absorbs into the bread.

4. Sprinkle generously with cinnamon or nutmeg.

5. Bake in a moderate to hot oven 160-180°C for 1 hour or until the custard is set.

6. Remove from oven and let stand for half an hour.

7. Generously dust with icing sugar and decorate with strawberry halves.

8. To serve, cut into squares and for individual serves, drizzle chocolate sauce on a large white plate. Place a serving of pudding in the middle of the plate, adding strawberries for decoration and re-dust with icing sugar just before serving.

Present

Fruit loaf works wonderfully well and helps your pudding rise because of the yeast in the bread. It also has the fruit and sultanas already in the bread, so it saves you adding these. An economical dish.

Cooked the day before, this dessert cuts easily and presents beautifully.

To reheat, simply microwave for 1 minute or more depending on size. It is perfect served with a dob of whipped cream, mascarpone cheese or ice cream.

Swirling the chocolate on the plate gives the finishing touches to this very simple and old family favourite.

This is Bob Maumill's favourite dessert. Ironic how he was telling me that he was forced to eat this growing up, and many of his listeners shared the same experience. What started out as a poor man's dessert, now graces the tables of many restaurants at a hefty price! I am pleased to say that Bob has told me, no word of a lie, that my Bread and Butter Pudding is the best he's ever tasted.

gracie mae!

Gracie Mae! Gracie Mae! We love the way
you cook and what you say!
Gracie Mae! Gracie Mae! We will love
your book and use it every day!

If you're looking for a lady, who's one cut above the rest,
In the field of all male butchers, the first one to pass the test,
And in the art of great home cooking, this top girl will always please,
With her knowledge of the kitchen and fantastic recipes.

With her Deli skills as back-ground, she knows meat from nose to tail,
How to cook a Chateau Briand, or a breast of tiny quail,
For salads, soups and seafood, grand desserts or simple sweets,
She knows everyday requirements plus those very special treats.

In a world that's getting faster, with so little time to spare,
She's a girl who'll always be there, her experience to share,
Her methods plain and simple, lead to quite delicious ends,
And you will surely be applauded by your family and friends.

Dr. Peter Harries
19 September 2011

EASY ENTERTAINERS

To some entertaining may be daunting, but it really can be easy to achieve an attractive looking and tasting meal. The secret is to follow my 4P's as explained in my introduction, guaranteeing you will arrive at my 5th P, **Perfection**.

Australians are notorious for their gatherings around the barbeque… "throw a shrimp on the barbie and she'll be right mate"…but I would like to show you how to "just whip up" an impressive but easy to create entertainer's package.

My guests often say, "Wow, you've gone to so much trouble, Grace." I inwardly smile because I know just how easy it was to put together a stunning spread. If only they knew what looks like hotel quality food is actually really very simple food presented with a touch of flair.

In this section I am giving you my trade secrets and I am confident that if you follow the plan you too will be able to say to your guests, "I just whipped it up."

The secret really is all in the presentation. The finishing touches, the garnishes are very important because they provide colour. Presenting food on different levels really also adds to the overall look of your 'spread'. If you don't have cake tiers, improvise. Turn a bowl upside down and put a cloth over it.

When it comes to garnishes, take a little extra care with these. Instead of cutting them plainly in slices, cut them on different angles. Choose colours that will contrast and add that splash of colour.

With finger foods it is great to have two or three different varieties on the same serving platters separating them by using small dishes (ramekins).

Food is very important when you are entertaining, but entertaining starts from the moment the guests arrive at your front door. You create the impression of what the event will be like.

For example, I hosted a large gathering for the editor and crew from a magazine at my home. They arrived and every woman was presented with a flower and their name was noted. Throughout the night my MC used their name in conversation and served them drinks. Everybody commented on the food, which of course was sensational, but you would be surprised how many commented on the fact that their name was remembered and that they received the flower.

The most important part of entertaining is to remember to make it fun. Stress free entertaining tops my list and with the element of fun thrown in, it's a complete winner.

I often invite a dear friend, Dr Peter Harries, to my special events. I enjoy his company and he also brings such joy to my guests when he sings, dances, entertains, tells jokes and raves about my cooking. It's the joy and banter that accompanies friendship that I most love.

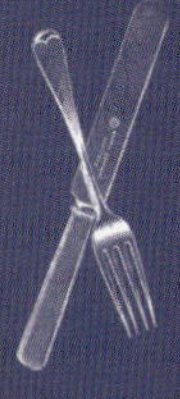

OH SO QUICK AND EASY PINWHEELS

Purchase

- 4 sheets ready roll puff pastry
- 500 gm mince (beef, chicken or pork)
- 2 eggs
- 1 cup bread crumbs
- 1 finely chopped onion
- 1 grated carrot
- ½ cup green and red capsicum, finely chopped
- ½ cup chopped parsley
- Salt & pepper for flavour

Prepare

1. In a large mixing bowl, place mince and all other ingredients. Mix well, making sure that meat is combined and binding together.

2. Lay pastry on board and divide the mixture evenly into 4 to cover the individual pastry sheets.

3. Spread the top of each pastry sheet with the mixture.

4. Gently roll pastry into long rolls.

5. Cut into 5 cm rounds and place on a baking tray lined with baking paper.

6. Bake in hot oven for 25-30 min or until pinwheels cooked.

Prepare

Serve in a basket; great entertainer food.

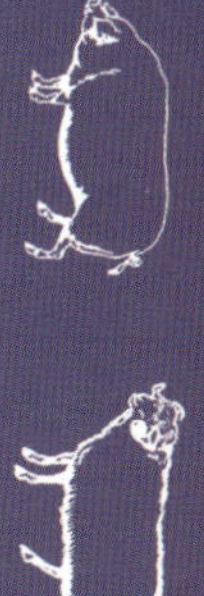

Purchase

2 racks of lamb or ask your butcher
for 12 French lamb cutlets

1 pkt bread crumbs
(herb and garlic flavoured)

½ cup fresh, chopped parsley

BBQ sauce for dipping

1 tbsp paprika

Salt and Pepper

Cooking oil

White paper frill (Grace style)

Prepare

1. In a flat glass dish, mix crumbs, chopped
   parsley, paprika, salt and pepper together.

2. Cut lamb rack into chops.

3. Dip each chop into the mixed crumbs,
   pressing very firmly so the crumbs stick to
   the lamb.

4. In a deep frying pan, place cooking oil,
   enough to fry each chop.

5. Brown the chops on each side.

6. Drain on baking paper.

7. Present chops on a round serving platter
   with a small dish filled with BBQ sauce in
   the middle.

8. Arrange chops evenly around the platter,
   with the bones sitting across the dipping
   bowl for ease of access. Place a paper frill
   on the end of one of the bones and place in
   the centre.

9. Decorate with swirls of BBQ sauce.

See page 85 for instructions on how to make the white paper frills

Present

You can add colour to the plate by adding a sprig of rosemary on the side.

These are perfect hot or cold.

HONEY SOY CHICKEN WINGS

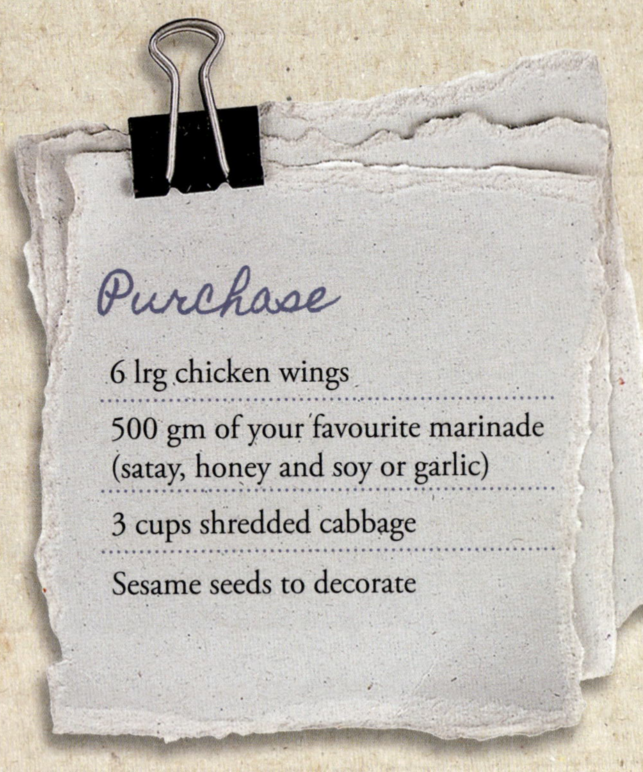

Purchase

6 lrg chicken wings

500 gm of your favourite marinade
(satay, honey and soy or garlic)

3 cups shredded cabbage

Sesame seeds to decorate

Prepare

1. Make two drummettes out of one wing by breaking wings at the centre joint and removing long thin bone. Pull down skins and cut in two.

2. Marinate with your favourite sauce (bottle or sachet) and pan fry for 8-10 mins until cooked through and golden brown.

3. Arrange on a bed of lettuce or thinly sliced cabbage and complement with dipping sauces – chilli or soy.

Present

Ideal as an entrée or for party nibbles.

It has taken me many years to understand what my father meant by saying, "Many a good broth is made from an old chook and many a good tune from an old fiddle." I now realise it has nothing to do with food or music, but rather with the fact that most things get better with age (men are like a good bottle of wine...they mature with age, he he he).

In the earlier years, and I'm sure a lot of butchers will relate to this story, a woman came to the butcher's counter and asked me to keep an eye on her shopping while she went back to pick up an item that she had forgotten. In the meantime, the mischievous part of me took over and I dashed out the back and removed an eye from a pigs head and placed it on the top of her shopping. When she returned, I heard this shriek and tried to keep a straight face. Horrified, she asked me, "What is this?" Innocently, I responded, "You did ask me to keep an eye on your shopping, didn't you?" Sadly, I could never understand why that was the last time I ever saw that lady.

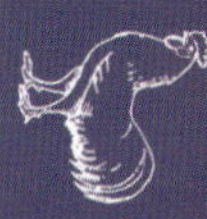

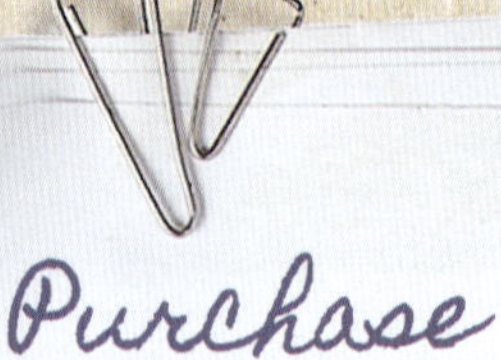

Purchase

2 lrg voul-au-vent shells

1 cup grated tasty cheese

1 cup cooked chicken breast fleeced

1 cup creamed corn

1 parsley sprig

Hungarian sweet paprika

1 cup of your favourite tasty mayonnaise

Prepare

1. In a deep bowl, combine chicken, corn, cheese and mayonnaise.

2. Mix well.

3. Scoop into voul-au-vent shells. Sprinkle with a little extra grated cheese and some paprika.

4. Bake in a hot oven 180-200°C for 10 mins.

5. Serve on a nice white serving dish.

6. Add parsley on the side and sprinkle paprika over the top and on the sides of the plate.

Present

Tuna can be used instead of chicken.

You can also use leftover meats combined with the above ingredients and this works very well.

I find this is one of the quickest and easiest dishes to put together in 10 mins.

I like to serve this with a tossed green salad and a glass of my favourite Chardonnay. If I can serve up a handsome young man as well, I'm delighted.

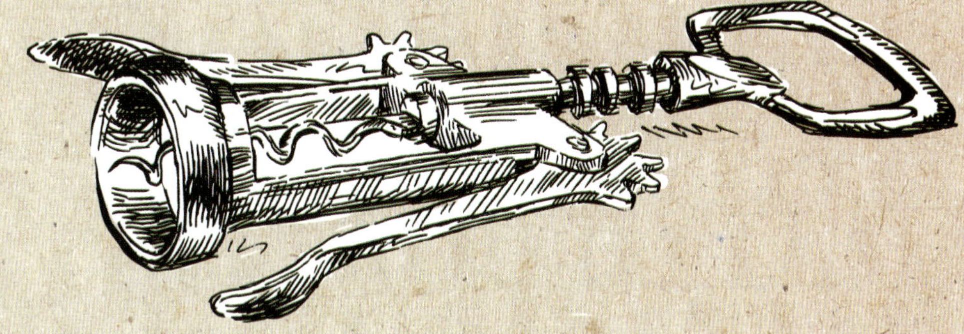

GRACE'S QUICK AND EASY PINEAPPLE SCONES

Purchase

2 pkts pre-made scone mix

2 tbsp castor sugar

1 tin pineapple pieces with juice

250 gm cold butter

½ cup lemonade

1 egg

Castor sugar to sprinkle on top and decorate

Present

For less mess on your muffin tin, place scone mix into muffin paper trays.

Serve with butter or pineapple rings.

A winner for the morning tea with your important friends or business associates. You'll be the most loved person at work if you bring these for morning tea!

Prepare

1. In a large mixing bowl, place the pre-made scone mix, castor sugar, and chop the cold butter into small cubes.

2. Combine the dry ingredients with the butter by using your finger tips to move the butter through the ingredients. Should have a crumbly finish.

3. Add the beaten egg, mixing well with a spoon.

4. Drain the tin of pineapple.

5. Add the lemonade and the pineapple pieces to the bowl.

6. Mix well, should be like a soft dough.

7. Use the pineapple juice if the mixture is a little dry. Be careful not to over wet the mixture.

8. Scoop into a greased muffin tin, equally sharing the mixture. This should make 12 large scones.

9. Sprinkle castor sugar generously on top. Scratch up the top to create a rough texture and place in a hot oven on 180°C for 40 minutes or until scones are golden brown and cooked through.

10. When scones are cooked, again sprinkle generously with castor sugar and let cool.

STRAWBERRY CRUSH

Purchase

4 punnets very lrg strawberries

Ice cubes

Prepare

1. Freeze strawberries overnight.
2. Choose a long stemmed large glass or glass dish.
3. Spoon ice cubes into the base of the glass or dish.
4. Make layers of frozen strawberries, placing ice cubes in between.

Present

Present this as a centrepiece for a dessert with a bowl of warmed chocolate for dipping.

These are also wonderful for a chocolate fondue, as frozen strawberries will set the chocolate.

Dipping the chilled strawberries in warm chocolate makes this a tantalisingly enjoyable and sexy dessert.

This also works well in a flatter deeper dish or individual martini glasses.

Friends and family get lots of pleasure in sharing recipes, meals and dining together. It's a great healthy way to be social as well.

QUICK AND EASY CHOCOLATE TREATS

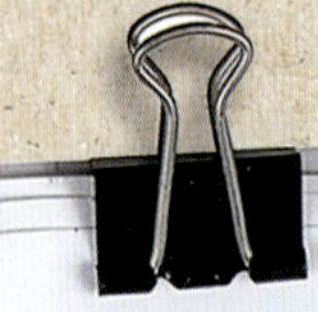

Purchase

1pkt pre-prepared chocolate shells (available in all different shapes and sizes from your continental deli or RE store)

1 punnet strawberries

Icing sugar for dusting

1 pkt chocolate drops

1 sachet pre-made custard in a piping bag or home made

Prepare

1. Fill chocolate shells with piping custard.

2. Place chocolate drops on each shell.

3. Dust with icing sugar and serve with strawberries on a tray.

Present

These can be pre-made and all ingredients have a decent shelf life, so is a good back up dessert or easy treat.

The perfect afternoon tea sensation for those who are time poor. I think you'll agree that these just look amazing and like you have gone to a lot of effort, yet are really effortless. "You'll love it!"

FRUIT COCKTAILS

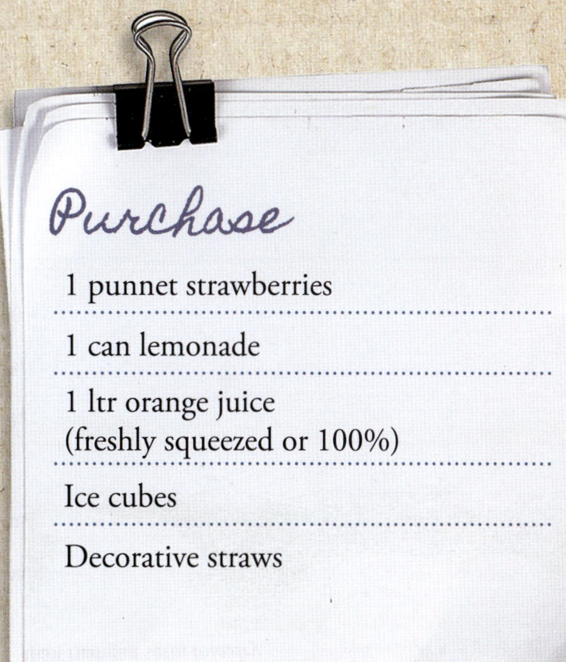

Purchase

1 punnet strawberries

1 can lemonade

1 ltr orange juice
(freshly squeezed or 100%)

Ice cubes

Decorative straws

Prepare

1. In two long chilled glasses, place 4 chopped strawberries and some ice cubes.
2. Divide the can of lemonade between the two glasses.
3. Top up with orange juice.
4. Add a decorative straw and stir.
5. Serve chilled.

Present

For a champagne breakfast, add a splash of champagne to the cocktail. Reduce the orange juice to accommodate the champagne.

Adding the lemonade to this cocktail reduces the acidity/bitterness of the orange juice, creating a fresh and invigorating flavour.

In summertime, I welcome my guests with a fruit cocktail, especially if we are gathered around the barbeque.

The addition of colourful decorative straws just seems to create that tropical island retreat feel and I love seeing the look of joy on my guests faces when they see the cocktails.

Chilling the glasses, either in the freezer or the refrigerator, prior to making the cocktail, reduces the need to refrigerate the cocktails prior to serving. You can literally make them and serve immediately and they are a lovely cool refreshing treat.

CUSTARD HORNS

Purchase

1 pkt pre-made custard horn shells

1 pkt red glazed cherries

1 sachet pre-made piping custard

Icing sugar for dusting

Mint leaves or artificial leaves for decoration

Prepare

1. Pipe custard into shells, filling generously.

2. Place a cherry on each end of the custard horn.

3. Generously dust with icing sugar.

4. Place on a large serving plate or tray and decorate with mint leaves or artificial leaves.

Present

These are best served as soon as filled.

Keeping the shells filled with custard overnight tends to make the shells soggy.

Perfect for that quick and easy dessert or served with short black Italian coffee.

An all-time favourite with my guests. I often serve with a liqueur or a Baileys and Cream.

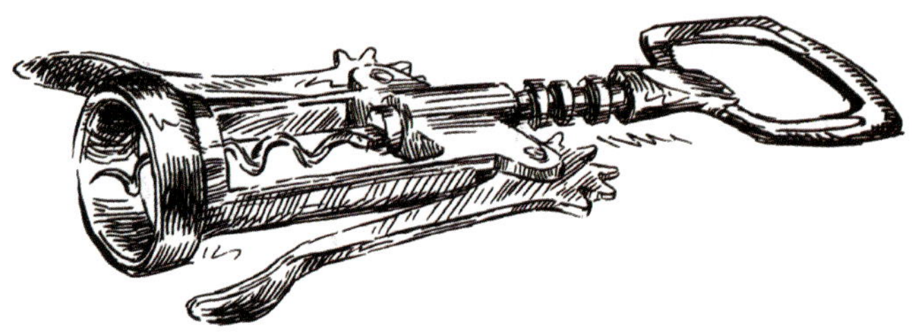

If the recipe or meal you have prepared for your dinner party doesn't turn out exactly as you expected, don't tell your guests. 90% of the time they won't even know.

FOODWORKS

Works for me!

**Edinburgh Road Shopping Centre,
Shop 1, 51 Edinburgh Rd,
FORRESTFIELD, WA, 6058**

Phone: 9453 3433

Opening Hours: 7 Days a Week Trading
Mon-Sat 7am-8pm
Sun 8am-8pm

GOOD VALUE • GOOD SERVICE • GOOD QUALITY • GOOD VARIETY

Pop in and meet The Butcher Who Bakes, Grace Maiolo, in person at Foodworks Fresh at Edinburgh Road Shopping Centre, 7am-12 noon.

Need a quick and easy meal, but are time limited?

We have freshly made, pre-packaged meals including curry and rice, spaghetti and meatballs, carbonara, schnitzels, sushi and Grace's jumbo gourmet sandwiches.

Located next to the 24 hour Fast Fuel depot.